Surfing Life's Waves

Reflections
for everyday life

By Jim Deeds

ISBN: 978-1-910044-07-0

Published in 2015 by Shanway Press, Belfast
www.shanway.com
email: info@shanway.com
T: 028 9022 2070

Cover design: Emma Heddles

Photographs supplied by Jim Deeds

About the author

Jim Deeds is a husband and a father from Belfast.
Jim currently works as co-ordinator of parish
development in the Diocese of Down and Connor, a
post he has held since 2012. During his 44 years,
Jim has also worked as busker, film maker, play-
wright, barman, glass washer, social worker, thera-
pist, manager of a children's home and an NHS
manager. It is this variety of life experiences and
his observations along the way that Jim brings to
bear in his writing, always looking for the spiritual
amongst the ordinary day to day. He enjoys
playing music now as a hobby and writing as a
healthy everyday addiction he hopes never to kick.

Foreword

I almost died surfing one time. It was back on January 2, 2007. I fell off my board in stormy waters and was held under for quite some time. I really thought I had bitten the big one. After a while I exploded upwards from the water and gulped in the precious air that awaited me. I struggled to shore and lay there exhausted until I got the energy up to make my way back to the car, get changed and go home. The rest of that day was a strange mix of pain (from holding my breath too long and getting battered by strong waves) and great thankfulness that I was alive. I remember that my vision seemed to be different that day and for a few days after. Things seemed brighter. Trees and plants and animals seemed ever more alive to me. Those I met all of a sudden took on more importance and looked more beautiful. My own existence looked a bit more precious.

I tell you all of this because it sums up pretty much what this book is all about: seeing things with our real eyes and seeing things as they really are. The reflections, poems and conversations contained here are attempts to see the good (I choose to call that God, but you don't have to) in all things; even, or maybe particularly, the difficult moments in life. That is why I've called this book, *Surfing Life's Waves*. Anyone who has ever surfed a wave knows that there are high points and low points in the wave. There's that sweet spot that, when you get on it, the surf is effortless and joyful. Then there are spots on the wave where it is a struggle to stay on the surf board. And of course, as all surfers know and accept, we fall... a lot! So, wherever you are on your life journey – a sweet spot, a difficult spot or a fall – I hope that there is something here that speaks to you.

Writing this foreword, I'm left wondering: 'How did this happen?' I didn't set out to write a book – let alone a book of reflections and poetry. Around February 2014, I decided that I would do something new for Lent: I'd write up on my Facebook page a simple prayer or something that I had seen that day. And so I did. I stuck to my Lenten promise and delivered 40 prayers and reflections (most are here in this book). Through the encouragement of my Facebook friends and family members, I continued to write and the strangest thing happened: I began to see things in each day that stood out to me as great moments of love or mercy or wisdom. I wrote them down; often discovering the words as I wrote them. The result is this book.

So, it is good to declare from the outset that I am a Catholic, a Christian and an imperfect work in progress (not necessarily in that order!) It is equally important to declare that I don't think you need to be any of these things to enjoy this book. I do not seek to preach or convert anyone through these words – simply to issue the invitation that I also give to myself each day to love more and more.

In terms of how the book is laid out or how it is to be read, you'll see that there are no chapters other than marking out the three styles of writing – reflections, poems and conversations. They are otherwise laid out as life itself is: in a mixed flow of topics. Flicking through and reading the titles of each reflection should give you a flavour of what it is about. I hope that by doing this you'll find the right words for you. I hope, also, that this book may be of some relevance to young people growing up.

So thank you to all who have encouraged and helped me through this process. In particular, as always, I owe a huge debt to my wife, Nuala and my children, Brendan, Joe and Eimear. I also owe John and all at Shanway a debt of gratitude for helping me to negotiate the waters of publication. And God. Thank God for everything.

Life is a wonderful ocean. Dive in!

Jim Deeds

Contents

Part one
The reflection section

Surfing life's waves

This is a picture of where I was one day for a couple of hours. It's White Rocks beach outside Portrush on the North Coast of Northern Ireland. I had two meetings up that end of the world and packed my surf board because I had some time to kill in between the meetings. Dodgy back and knees notwithstanding, I did well and enjoyed every wave.

The world can be a busy old place. The busy-ness of life can be all consuming. But that's not the whole story. There are moments of sacred space to be had in the middle of the busy-ness. I had one such moment today – my time on White Rocks beach. Sacred space is full of possibilities. It can be filled with all manner of things. Today, I filled it with surfing, thinking and praying. It did my body, mind and I think my soul good.

At times I was almost moved to tears looking at the wonder of God in nature and experiencing something of God's power in the power of the waves.
In the pull back and forward of the current I reflected on the different directions I am pulled in at the moment. I experienced the conflicting feelings and opinions I have on some situations in my life and I asked for strength to let go of my need for control.

In surfing the waves I experienced the possibility of rising above problems and worries and letting God carry me along.

In watching the tide rise along the beach I reflected on the certainty of God and the fact that, just as the tide comes in and goes out, God too has a rhythm and a plan and a direction for each life.

As I sat on the beach looking out to sea I saw the other surfers in the water- some just starting to surf; others nearing the end of their time surfing. I got a sense of all of us together in life at different stages. Some young in years and some old in years. Of myself getting older in years but still young at heart and, like a child, still in need of guidance and support.

Sacred space can be where you find it. Today I found it on the beach. Your sacred space is waiting for you to (re)discover it. I pray that when you do, it is filled with every grace and blessing.
Amen

For the wounds we carry

I have three scars that carry stories of my life. One is in the centre of my forehead (and is lost under the wrinkles: themselves a story of my journey to middle age). I got it when I was two years old. We had moved to our family home in Arizona Street six months previously and the newness of the house coupled with the unsteadiness of a toddler's gait led me to trip on a step and split my head open. Growing up my mum often told of the panic that ensued as her first born bled and screamed like life was over. The local nurse was called for and put paper stitches on my head and all was well. The scar and the story of the wound has travelled with me to this day.

The second scar is on the bottom right side of my left palm. It's a round scar I got from a wound received after a fall competing in the long jump on the gravel covered tarmac of St Teresa's Youth Club summer scheme around 1984. The cut got infected and a long thin red line sprouted from it and travelled up my arm. A sign of blood poisoning I believe. A trip to the hospital ensured and an embarrassing need to drop my trousers to a female nurse for her to administer a tetanus shot. The feeling of vulnerability and embarrassment is still palpable today.

The third is really so small it's hardly a scar. It's the mark left on my right knee after a meniscectomy – the removal of part of the meniscus (the cartilage in my knee) by keyhole surgery. This came after a period of eight months on crutches and strong pain killers. This scar reminds me of suffering and being disconnected from myself. It also reminds me of the day after surgery when I walked unaided to the local shops (three whole minutes away!) and the sense of freedom that came with it.

Our woundedness is not limited to physical wounds of course. Emotional wounds can cut deeper and I'm not sure I'd be able to write here in an open forum my top three emotional scars if I'm really honest. That said all wounds tell a story. Often they tell of pain and even horror. But they can also tell of our life journey, the people who accompanied us through the pain and even of redemption (like my first unaided walk to the shops).

May we have the courage and strength to acknowledge our own woundedness in the hope that we may see the redemption in the midst of the pain. May we not pass on our woundedness to others. May we see those who are wounded and join them in their woundedness seeking to heal when we can and simply journeying with them when we can't.

Amen

Gifts hidden

Us folk in Norn Iron (Northern Ireland to those of you who don't speak the lingo) aren't great at shouting about our gifts and talents. We hide our lamp under the bed so to speak. Yet everyday you:

Support sick people
Put up patiently with criticism
Love your husbands/wives/significant others
Carry out the difficult tasks your jobs require
Tell jokes
Cook
Play games
Listen to those who need an ear
Make things
Write beautiful poems
Sing and play music
Grow plants and flowers
Pray
Draw and paint
Debate and discuss
And on and on.....

So tonight I pray in thanksgiving for your gifts and talents. Even if you don't like to shout about them (or maybe don't even see them) I want to honour them and the One who gave you them.

A reflection for tonight could be:
'our gifts are given to us so that we may in turn give them away in acts of love, kindness, compassion and mercy'
May your light continue to shine.
Amen

Kenosis

Kenosis – the emptying of myself and the unhelpful attachments I have (money, possessions, pride, guilt, what else?)

I once applied for a job for all the wrong reasons. People told me I'd be good at it. The pay was well above what I had ever earned before. I would get to make decisions (be in control). In other words I applied for the job not because I had a passion for the work but because the idea stroked my ego.

I took the job. I wore a suit (can you believe it?!) and 'played the part'. It didn't go well. I didn't really know what I was doing. My bosses wanted me to do things that didn't sit well with me. Some of the staff I managed were kinda savage and they ate me up (I'm a softy). I began to die inside. I became sick.

Life dealt me the situation where I had to let go. I faced the humiliation of admitting I wouldn't go back. I had failed. I saw failure as a negative thing (not as part of every journey as I do now) and I became very down. I took time off and tried to heal.

And then it began to happen. I began to re-look; at myself, at life, at everything. I walked a lot. I sensed that I was emptying myself of the negative feelings that had built up. I began to empty myself of my stories of who I was and what I 'should' be. I began to breathe. I began to get fit. I began to pray more and go regularly to weekday Mass (first to plead for help, then to thank God for the help I was getting). I healed and went back to work (in a different job).

That experience of emptying myself created space for the little conversions we all need daily. It got me thinking more and, looking back, was an important time for my spiritual development (although most of that time I felt stressed and depressed and useless). The lesson of that emptying of myself and the distancing from the ego is one I've forgotten and re-learned many times since (although not so clearly or dramatically as that time).

I now know that as long as I strive to be an 'empty vessel', the process of emptying myself allows me to be filled by Another. And when that emptying happens I feel more alive; more filled up. Go figure!

May we come to know the Love that fills us more than anything else. May we make room for peace, love, justice and service. And may we know that no matter what we have done or who we are God needs only a little space in our lives to fill us up.
Amen

God is in everything or else God is in nothing

Let's all think on this. It challenges all of us I would say.

If God is in everything, then God is in all those things and people we keep at a distance. God is in the moments of difficulty as well as the moments of ease. God is in our mistakes as well as our right choices.

For us Catholics we believe (don't we?) that God is made real in the Eucharist. But it doesn't end there. God is just as real in me after communion (the 'you are what you eat' principle). This, surely, has implications for how I view and treat myself. God is in the people I meet through the day- no matter what their faith (or no faith) stance, their political beliefs, their sexuality, their marital status, their past actions, their view of me. God is in everything. Or God is in nothing.

I respect that some of my buddies can answer the top question by clearly saying God is in nothing. I can't (it's not even that I don't want to - I can't say God is in nothing). And because I can't say God is in nothing, I have to say God is in everything.

That means that I am constantly challenged to look and look again at how I live my life; at how I view my purpose in life; and how I have blind spots about individuals and groups of people who I don't talk about or act towards as if God were in them. And yet, the challenge of looking again brings possibilities of seeing the world through different eyes (God's eyes). And having seen it that way, of acting out of that vision. I'm up for that challenge. Who will join me?
Amen

The 'refresh package'

A while ago I sent a guitar back to the manufacturers after many years of it being a working guitar – playing in streets busking, bars gigging and churches worshipping. The years had taken their toll. It was lacklustre. There was a crack in the top. The electrics had stopped working. The company gave it the 'refresh package'. It came back looking, feeling and playing like new.

Can I tell you something? I'm a bit like that guitar at the minute. I'm a bit tired and feeling lack lustre. I'm going to take a trip to Lagos in Portugal as a 'refresh package'. Physically, emotionally and spiritually nourishing. I've got a bike lined up to go out riding every day. I'm going to spend lots of time with my wife and kids. I'm going to visit the wonderful village churches around Lagos. I'm gonna read scripture and books that feed my soul. And I'm gonna pray.

May we all be blessed with opportunities to get a 'refresh package'. At home or abroad. It's a good idea.
Amen

Struggling through adversity

I met a woman one day who I had the privilege of looking after when she was a child and I was a young residential social worker 20 or so years ago. She had a difficult start in life to put it mildly and had to fend for herself from age 16 on. Today I saw her with one of her three beautiful children; a wonderful mother and a kind person. She is remarkable and I felt the benefit of spending a few short minutes with her catching up. I'm blessed to know a lot of adults like this woman.

May all children have the Care and Protection they need. And when they don't and have to struggle through may we who see them know that they are working ten times harder to achieve what most of us take for granted.
Amen

Simple living

I often get caught up in so many things that distract me from what is important in my life. Our lives can become unnecessarily complicated. We can elevate trivial things to positions of great (and unwarranted) importance. When this happens we can become disconnected from family or friends or prayer life.

May all of us take time each day and connect to what is really important and Life Giving to us.

Amen

The quiet ones

There are many people in our lives who are quietly helping us on our journeys; easing the load or burden. Often their acts of help are small (but right on the mark). Sometimes it's not until we stop to think about who we have in our lives that we notice these people and how their help builds us into the people we can be.

May we notice those who help us on our way. And may we thank them when we do, telling them how much they mean to us. And may we in turn look for the small ways we can ease the burden for others and build them up along their journey.

Amen

One, two, three

Tonight as you settle down, call to mind 1,2,3.

One moment of difficulty today that you would like to see resolved
Two moments of joy, happiness, contentment, beauty (really push yourself here to find something)
Three people you could show love, generosity, forgiveness, patience to tomorrow.

May we be graced to resolve our difficulties; be thankful for those moments of joy and beauty; and be strong in our efforts to reach out in love to others. And may God bless us all.

Amen

Thanksgiving for laughter

It's been a LONG weekend. I've been in a monastery, a priory and two Churches. I've spoken at two Masses and worked with representatives of four Parish Pastoral Councils and one Pastoral Area team. I appreciate that to some of you here that may mean nothing but safe to say I've been around a lot of people and doing a lot of work. No complaints or sympathy called for though because it was all great. That said, it was tiring.

So I want to give thanks for a moment of laughter this afternoon. I was with my good friend Paddy Linden and we shared a moment of schoolboy humour. The laughter started and then went on. And on. And on. The tears rolled down my face and I felt refreshed, rejuvenated, reconnected to my self and my soul. It reminded me of the countless other times that I've laughed with friends over the years.

Life can be busy. And life can be very sad and worrying. But (or even because of this) we can still find times for laughter and silliness.

May we take time to see the humour around us. May we other people and help them to laugh. And may God continue to provide moments of schoolboy (and schoolgirl!) humour for us on our journey.
Amen

P.S. thanks Paddy.

For dough (stick with me here)

Bread dough, once mixed, is left in a dark place and in a short time has doubled in size. But then, before it can become bread, the dough is knocked back a bit- it's worked with and kneaded- until the air is taken out of it and it becomes smaller and we are able to create something nourishing out of it.

Small hurts become big hurts when we leave them inside or don't acknowledge/talk about them. They can begin to assume more power over us than they need to. They can feel too big to deal with and overwhelm us. They need to be knocked back a bit. And yet, even at the stage when the hurt has multiplied beyond where it needed to go, the process of knocking it back – of talking to others about it or going to the root cause of the hurt or simply letting it go – can still provide the possibility of creating something better. It can create God's possibility of healing. And that can feed us and those around us who are witnesses to the healing.

May we recognise hurts in us and those around us. May we be graced with the ability to deal with hurts when they are small and when they are big. May we seek forgiveness from those we have hurt. And may we see the resolution of difficult situations as opportunities to make something nourishing that can feed us.
Amen

Turning points

Every so often in life we come to a junction. It may be a time when a decision is required that we know will take us on a new journey or direction.

It may be that we have concluded a new direction is needed and we have sought it out. Or it may be that life throws us a curve ball and all of a sudden things change. This last one might come at us as something challenging. Or even as something uninvited, unwelcome and troubling.

Whichever it is, may we know that there is a plan greater than our own. That in the chaos or the troubled times God is with us. And may we know that if we keep ourselves open to the ways of love and selflessness, God will guide us towards a tuning point that takes us on the right path.
Amen

Standing in a new place

I attended a religious service this morning in St Anne's Cathedral. It was a service in a different tradition to mine. It was in a Cathedral with imagery and flags not of my tradition or of my community growing up. It was along with people who, until this last year, I didn't know and didn't see myself knowing.

It was one of the most moving experiences I've had in a long time. There was a deep respect for tradition and, better still, of difference. So, it got me thinking.

Life looks different when we go and stand in a new place. It may be attending a religious service in another denomination. It may be visiting an area once seen as belonging to 'the other side'. It may be recognising hurt in people once demonised. It may be trying to imagine yourself in the situation of someone you see yourself standing in judgement of. Whatever it is (and there are countless opportunities for this – I've chosen very 'Northern Ireland' suggestions), today reminded me that it's worth doing.

In that new space we meet new possibilities of growth, learning, love and reconciliation. In that space, I say, we meet God.

But be careful, in that space we are utterly changed. And in some way, the world looks a little brighter.

May we experience the invitation to stand in a new place. And when we are invited, may we respond positively.
Amen

For those who feel it's all uphill

I was walking along the River Lagan this morning and was bowled over by the beauty of nature. I was filled with wonder and contentment that I was there.
And then I came across this scene. A path up a hill. Something about it drew me to stop. I stood and looked up the path. I looked at the steps up the hill and this reflection came to me.

Life can feel like it's all uphill sometimes: like every moment takes more energy or commitment than we have to give to it. We can get caught out looking too far ahead and become dizzy thinking about the heights we will have to scale going up the hill. In doing this we fail to see the beauty all around the hill.

And yet we could see life as more of a series of steps rather than one continual, never ending hill. Each step can provide a moment of rest. A moment to pray. A moment to take stock. If we concentrate on just one or two steps at a time and take the time in between to rest and pray and be thankful for making the small steps, we can slowly make our way up the hill. And in doing so we won't need to look too far ahead. We won't need to get dizzy. We won't miss the beauty along the way.

May we see small steps rather than unscalable hills. May we find those struggling up hill and invite them to join us for a rest on one of life's steps. And may we see the beauty around us on the way.
Amen

Finding beauty in the middle of imperfection

My friend Paddy Linden gave me a record player last weekend. I haven't owned a record player in 25 years at least. I've spent the last week waiting for a small part that was missing to arrive from good old eBay. Today it came and the record player was complete. What joy! I dug out my old records from my mum's house and marvelled at how big they are compared to the CDs we have now (which are infinitely physically bigger than the downloaded music my kids listen to). Seeing the old records brought back so many memories for me. It was really wonderful.

I put on the first record and heard the whirr of the motor as it moved the needle into place. And then came a sound I had all but forgotten – the scratch! Remember? The scratch of the needle across the vinyl. And then the slow thump noise as the record spun. A kind of rhythm of its own. All of this going on underneath the sound of the music. At once at variance with the natural rhythm and melody of the music, yet also completing the experience of listening to the music. I was overwhelmed in a nostalgic haze (purple, of course!).

So much of the content and nature of our lives is imperfect. In our eyes as well as the eyes of others. There are scratchy noises and thumps in our lives where we and others wish there was only beautiful music. A lot of the time we can get caught up in only seeing the imperfections. And while often real, the imperfections also occur, sometimes, in the context of real beauty.

Take for example the death of a loved one. Recently, my father in law died. God rest his soul. The pain I saw my wife go through (and the pain of her siblings and family) was one of life's imperfections. I wanted it to go away. It was a 'scratchy noise' in all of our lives and it hurt badly. And yet, in the midst of this imperfect situation I was privileged to witness a family who pulled together; a family who immersed themselves in the religious and spiritual elements of the funeral; a family who loved. Such beauty in the midst of imperfection.

Take for example the brother who does not believe in God, but who cares so deeply about his children and his family; who will go the extra mile to see that justice is done; who knows that what Jesus said was powerful. I can get caught up in the imperfection (as I see it in my moments of judgement, God forgive me) of his belief systems. Or I can marvel at the beauty of his passion for people and invite him into my belief system – invite mind you, not demand.

You will have your own examples. It's not to say that we seek imperfection. But, I guess, we accept it when we encounter it. We realise that we, also, are imperfect in so many ways. And we re-commit ourselves to looking to the beauty of life where it really lies.

May we all have the insight to see our own imperfections before those of others. May we have the humility to realise that we are all called to perfect our imperfections where we can. And may we seek only to journey with all people where they are at, in perfect love of them.

Amen

Special children

There are special kids who have to work that bit harder to understand their world but who bring so much joy and inspiration to those of us privileged enough to watch them do it. For all children with autism, Asperger's, ADHD, ASD. For their parents and families and friends. We pray for their relationships to be a witness of the great gift of God's love among us.

Amen

Those suffering from depression

The thick blanket of sadness, low feelings, worthlessness, negativity (almost always turned in on the self), or just no feeling at all that comes with depression can debilitate the person. May they come to know their true worth. May they see themselves as God sees them – a perfect creation, a thing of beauty and a blessing to the world. May we who know them bless them with kind words and loving actions.

Amen

All sick children

Those in hospital and those at home. We pray that they are comforted, healed and loved. We pray also for those who care for them. Their parents and carers and family. And especially for those who dedicate their lives to the care and protection of sick children- doctors, nurses, social workers and staff of all types who give of their time and energy.

Amen

For anyone in conflict

Prayers tonight for anyone who finds themselves in conflict with friends, family, partners. Sometimes misunderstanding or harsh words spoken in haste take on a life of their own and can lead to hard feelings, hurt or relationships breaking down. Once loving friendships become silent and barren. May all who are in conflict find a path to Peace and Forgiveness in the knowledge that connections between people are precious and privileged and need to be nurtured. Sometimes this means saying sorry- even if we don't want to or think we shouldn't have to.

Amen

Young people

It's not easy growing up (I think I'm still in the middle of it!). Life throws a lot at our young people and many fall casualty to excess, poor support or bad decisions. Still others are a beacon of hope for us as they plot their way through life with energy and passion. May our young people have the Love they need to grow safely and wisely. May society look out and after them and may those who have grown beyond being young look to them for inspiration, remembering always that we made some pretty dodgy decisions ourselves on the way up.

Amen

Homeless

Prayers on this cold, wet and windy Belfast night for those people who find them-selves homeless and on the street. One of the basic needs we have as humans is to have a secure base; a place of safety; a roof over our heads. Walking through the city streets we see so many empty buildings boarded up, unused. And yet in those same streets there are people huddling in doorways. Some are quick to label or judge them. Thank God others are out there to help them. May they all come to have a Se-cure place to live, survive and thrive.

Amen

Grandparents

Prayers today for grandparents. The picture is of my granda Jimmy Webb. He died in 2001. Grandparents can bring a sense of calm and wisdom to those who know them. Jimmy Webb was one such person. He built me into the man I am (the good bits anyway. The rest is my own fault). May grandparents experience the Love and Respect they deserve and may those who still have grandparents know the bless-ing that they are.

Amen

Police and law and order

Prayers tonight for police and those charged with upholding law and order. Nuala and I were out for dinner tonight and on our way home we saw a young man steal-ing from people outside a bar. He ran away and about 50 yards later was tripped up and held by another man. This man called for help and it became clear that he was a cop. Other cops came and took the man back to where he had stolen from the peo-ple outside the bar. They were firm with him but not aggressive thank God.

May those who have the difficult job of helping victims of crime always act out of justice and fairness. May others, in turn, treat police with fairness.

Amen

New life and the possibilities of healing

I was at a birthday party for a great young man who had reached 18. His granny died on this day eight years ago. On his 10th birthday. Birthdays have been difficult for him. And there have been other difficult moments for him since that. However, this night he was at the gateway of adulthood and even though I know he misses his granny, he is also happy. May we know that there is always possibility of hope and healing after loss and grief. Happy birthday Conor!

Amen

For all undertaking exams

Over the course of the year there will be many children, young people and adults studying away and sitting exams. Some will find it easy. Others will find it difficult. And some will find it almost impossible (perhaps because of responsibilities, stresses or worries they have that get in the way).

May they all do the best they can. And may they know that no exam result can be the judge of any person. St Joseph of Cupertino pray for them all.

Amen

For good things

Praying right now for nothing but good things for you all. I pray that whatever is causing you stress and worry is resolved. I'm praying that those people close to you show their love to you in very real ways and that you show them your love (first if needs be). I'm praying that good health continues and that poor health improves. I'm praying that hopes are fulfilled and fears were never based in reality anyway. I'm praying for you.

Amen

God can't steer a parked car

Reading, thinking, reflecting – all great things. But better when they lead to action. What one thing could you commit to doing today that would be an expression of love? Could you go out of your way (even out of your comfort zone) to reach out in help or service to someone? Could you smile and say nothing, even when the  temptation would be to blow your top? Could you make contact with someone who might need a friendly voice or hug?

Action allows God to steer the car. Let's act.
Amen

I'm still a work in progress

Prayers tonight for the reminders that I'm still a work in progress. Most days I get a reminder in the form of moments of anger, prejudice, despair, jealousy, greed, selfishness. And that's a good day!

May I notice these reminders and the direction they are setting me in my search for holiness (wholeness). May I not spell them away nor resent them. May I not go too easy on myself so as to stilt any growth nor too hard on myself as this will do the same thing. And may I continue to seek Guidance on the way.
Amen

An encounter with God

The readings at mass one day reminded me of two things. Firstly, it is wrong to take advantage of people. In particular the first reading from Amos warned against wheeling and dealing to get a few pounds out of people. Against loan sharking. Against plotting to keep the poor poor and the rich rich. We live in a disposable culture at times. People can often be seen as stepping stones for others to stand on to get higher up the ladder. Amos speaks of the injustice of such a culture.

The Gospel reading from Matthew reminded me that everyone is capable of transformation when they encounter God. Matthew the tax collector has dinner with

Jesus and this transforms his life. The Pharisees look on and condemn Jesus for eating with sinners (imagine!). But Jesus gently meets Matthew and Matthew has a life changing moment.

Where will we be open enough today to encounter God? In the beautiful natural world around us? In Church? In our family and friends? Keeping ourselves open enough (and not shutting down or judging like the Pharisees did) to believe we can encounter God seems to allow us to do just that – see God in... well everything!

Some challenges:
Give a homeless person some money or food when you see them today
Consider giving regularly to a charity for the poor
Invite your relatives and friends to do likewise
Where you see injustice ask what you can do to reverse it
Keep your eyes open today for the goodness in your life
(even in the midst of hardship)
Sit with those moments of goodness and contemplate whether they are an expression of God in this world
Be amazed by beauty
Speak gently when you don't feel like it
End the day with a prayer – your own words or a prayer you know/remember

Know that you are loved (sit with that one for a while and watch it begin to chip away at all the reasons you made up to tell yourself that you're not)
Amen

An oasis

This is a picture of my daughter Eimear's class project. It's an oasis in the middle of a desert. It got me thinking today about both the desert times in our lives and of the oases we find if we are open to finding them.
The desert times can be manifold, can't they? We experience them in the midst of grief, trauma, job loss, relationship difficulty and more. The desert can feel different for different people.

Some of us feel,
useless
worthless
frustrated
empty
angry
depressed

We can feel life is just a hassle and the world cruel. At these times, God can feel very far away and prayer is next to impossible. Perhaps, if not praying people, we feel that no other person in the world can or wants to understand us. Just as a desert is unbearably hot during the day and freezing cold at night, our times of being in the desert in our lives can burn us with pain, cynicism and self doubt. They can then freeze us in our relationships with others and ourselves, and make us feel 'out in the cold' compared with the rest of the world. I don't know about you but I've been in the desert many times. 40 days and 40 nights times ten you might say!
Most of us haven't had the experience of being lost in a physical desert. Of walking for miles and miles without water or rest. But let's take a moment and imagine what that would be like. Imagine seeing a sight like the one our Eimear has recreated: pools of water and shade in the midst of pain, suffering, hopelessness. Imagine the coolness of the water we would drink. Water that gave us real life. Water that quenched our thirst and gave us hope for a better life.

Sometimes gradually, sometimes suddenly, sometimes alone, sometimes through the support and guidance of others (but always surprisingly) I've come to a break in my desert times- an oasis. Times where I thought there was no hope and where the pain would not end turned into moments of relief, of hope and of possibility.
Take a moment and think about the times of oasis in your life. Really do this. When were these times? Call to mind the places you found an oasis in life (I find it in Rossnowlagh, in Tobar Mhuire (Passionist monastery in Crossgar), in the Falls Park, on Davis Mountain). Who brought you oasis in your life (I think of my wife Nuala, of my parents, of real friends). Think of how it felt to be in this place of oasis. Think of the peace it brought you.

The oasis will not be found in alcohol, drugs, sex, possessions, control, status. The oasis will rarely be found alone. To find the oasis we will need others (and so we can lead others to their oasis). The oasis lies in finding our true selves. In connecting to our core- our Spirit. For me, the oasis is only found through letting go of the ego and acknowledging that I, alone, am not enough. That I am part of a bigger whole. And of connecting to the bigger whole through prayer to God who holds us all.

May we come to know that the desert times are not the whole picture and that there will be times of oasis. May we reach out to those in desert times and invite them into the oasis of love, service and understanding. May we look outside ourselves for the answers to life's questions. And may God protect and bless us all this night.
Amen

The lessons we learn in the most unusual places

I had occasion to be in a waiting area this morning. Whilst there, I decided to indulge my coffee habit. I moved to the coffee machine, inserted my pound and waited as the brown stimulant was poured. Duly delivered I waited for the change. Ten seconds later the 10p change shot out of the machine like a bullet. Straight out of the machine, past me and underneath the machine next door. Hmm... What to do? Being a man interested in justice (but cute enough to look around to see that no one was watching) I bent down to look for said coin. In the process I saw two things. Namely, the ten pence was far out of reach and, joy of joys, there was a TWENTY pence piece lying on the floor well within reach. Fair dues, I thought, and lifted the 20p. I sat down to enjoy my coffee and my 'winnings'. Sitting there, I couldn't work out what burned more: the coffee in my hands or the ill gotten gains in my pocket. 'That 20p belonged to some other poor soul robbed by the errant machine', I thought.

And so, with a healthy dose of the old Catholic guilt, I resolved to put the 20p in the poor box or give it to someone less fortunate than I.

Another hour passed and the craving for coffee kicked in again. And so, with more determination this time, I approached the machine.
'Not this time machine. I know your game.'

I repeated the steps: pound in, button pressed, coffee out. This time, though, I put my hand over the hole whence the last 10p was launched. And then I waited. And waited. And...a beep. The sign on the machine read: 'no change available'. I had been vanquished by the coffee dispenser. In the almost silent waiting area I swear I heard a faint laugh emanating from the coffee machine.

I sat down. The coffee was.... just alright.
I found the 20p coin. 'I broke even', I initially thought. Ten pence up. Then ten pence down. But it still burns a hole. 20p anyone?

May we all keep a sense of perspective and laugh even when defeated (by machines or others). May we remember the value of money for our and others' lives. And may we seek to give away as much as or more than we seek to gather in.

Amen

For standing in relationships

Every now and then we become aware of just how much life is about relationship. This will typically be in one of two situations.

Firstly, at those times when we are so overwhelmed by the loving actions of someone towards us in a time of great need. Spend a minute and think of a time in your life when you truly were at the edge of something that took away your sense of security; your sense of yourself even.

Now call to mind the person or the people who were there for you at that time. Call to mind the small or great things they did with and for you. Call to mind the moments of sharing your worries you had with these people and the comfort their simple acts of relationship brought you.

The second times are those when we see suffering in another and are moved to be with them. Call to mind a friend or relative or even a stranger you saw in sorrow, pain, suffering. Remember the burn of injustice you felt for them. Now remember the small things you did: a smile, a listening ear, a hug, practical support.

Whether you know it or not these actions carried God's possibility of bringing great comfort to that person.

May we remember the value of relationships in life. May we remember in thanksgiving the people who have brought us comfort by relating to us. And may we never underestimate the difference we can make by choosing to stand in relationship with others.

Amen

Being a perpetual beginner

When I first started to learn the guitar, I remember the newness of it. The excitement of it. The possibility of it. And I found it very seductive. Every day I craved time with the guitar. I play every day still but back then it seemed that I needed to spend hours every day with the guitar. I remembered with a friend at the weekend that after the age of 17 (when I got my first guitar) I stopped buying records (I still don't have much of a collection of CDs and stuff) because all my money went on the guitar – strings, plectrums (plectra?!), straps, amps and then on more guitars. I knew I wasn't great. But hey, I was only a beginner and that was OK. I'd get into it as I practised.

A beginner's enthusiasm is something to behold. I see it in my daughter as she begins secondary school. All the new subjects and homework. A certain energy she didn't have at the end of primary school. I've seen it in a new member of the team in work this year. I've been inspired by it as I accompany a relative on beginning the journey of fighting ill health.

Someone said to me (and I hear this every night somewhere out in our Church groups that I work with) that she felt she had nothing to offer because she was so inexperienced in matters of 'God'. We're often caught up measuring ourselves by the experience of others in all sorts of walks of life.

And yet when it comes to God (whatever way you experience God), there are only beginners. There are no people further up the hill than others. Because there is no hill. No competition. No comparisons. No rungs on the ladder of success. No ladder at all. Only beginners, seeing through a glass, darkly. Seeing God with the eyes of children- the ultimate beginners – seems to be the way we see God best. And even then it's only an approximation of all that God is – and a poor approximation at that I'd bet. So I pray that I may retain the beginner's enthusiasm. The beginner's humility. The beginner's knowledge that I'm always at the start of something new, with plenty to learn. That life always will be something best seen and approached with a child's eyes. And that when I stuff things up- hey I'm a beginner. I'll ask for forgiveness, regroup and start again.

Suddenly, things that may have felt like a terrible end- in work, in friendships, in love, in health (and ultimately, death) – may simply be invitations to new beginnings. Now that's an invitation I can say 'yes' to!

May we see every new day as a new beginning. May we embrace each person we know and meet as fellow beginners and see their mistakes as necessary learning points; not merely annoyances for us. May we never make others feel like beginners in the company of 'experts'. And may God bless and protect us all as we enter another new moment of beginning again. Right now!

Amen

Purposeful words

A friend told me a story yesterday about words. He worked for a time as a hospital chaplain and every day he visited people who were ill in bed. He talked and prayed with them. After a while he noticed the amount of activity the nursing and medical staff undertook with the same patients. He saw the medicine administered; the xrays taken; the wounds bandaged. He came to question his contribution. 'I'm only saying a few words'. He remembered feeling a bit useless.

He then told me of his time (after being a chaplain) of teaching a class of 10-year-olds. During this time, he could see the attention the pupils paid to homework requests; to praise; to admonishment. All spoken words.

He concluded by telling me that from then on he has come to know the power of the spoken word.

The words we use are precious. But most of us most of the time talk until we have something to say. We often use words frivolously, without purpose. And yet, try this. Call to mind your times of being hurt in life. Now call to mind the times of being built up in your life. Would it be fair to say that a lot of those times involved things people said to you? Yep. For me too.

Words can carry our purpose. They can be tools for doing good or weapons for destroying people at their core. Using words purposefully we can let people know they are:
Doing good
Loved
Welcome
Going in a direction that is not good for them
Not alone
Beautiful
The product of a thought of God

May we come to know the potential of the spoken word. May we develop an understanding of what our purpose is. And may we use our words wisely, furthering our purpose.
Amen

The twists and turns in the road

Life is full of surprises isn't it? Some more welcome than others of course. At times, we can feel like we're on the straight and narrow and then... oops! Life twists and turns and we're off in another direction.
The twists and turns bring hidden challenges to us:
We're doing well in work. Then something comes up and we have to put in extra hours or take on extra duties.

The kids are doing well and then they fall out with friends and they need us to give them extra time and attention.

The parents are keeping the best. Then one or both become old and frail and we need to reverse roles and take care of them.
Our relationship with our significant other is sweetness and light. Then the hard times hit and we question if we've made the right decision.

We're sure of our path in life. Then doubt strikes and we wonder if it's all been in vain.

The twists and turns can be disconcerting and frightening for us. They can leave us anxious, confused and cynical.

But let's look again:
The curve ball in work allows us to develop our skills, understand (the limitation maybe of) our roles and gives us the opportunity to ask for help.

The kids' dilemmas allow us to spend more time with them and accompany them on valuable life lessons. Our parents' illness, though saddening, allows us to pay back the care they gave to us and to be a source of love and care for them.

The difficulties in our relationship give us the opportunity to work through them selflessly and to discover hidden strengths in our love for ourselves and each other.

Our life direction crisis gives us the opportunity to re-evaluate our purpose in life and to ask ourselves where we're truly meant to be.

The twists and turns are difficult at times but I believe that behind each twist and turn we find as many opportunities as challenges. We can find despair. But we can also find God, constantly inviting us to grow in love and maturity. Much of this depends on how we choose to see things and how our companions in life help us to see things.

A wise friend told me recently, 'it's a long road that has no turns'. I didn't know what she meant to be honest. But thinking about it now I take from that phrase that a road without twists and turns would look very long indeed and faced with such a long road we may not set out on a journey at all. And what a loss that would be.

May we face the twists and turns in life with a sense of their opportunities as well as their challenges. May we find God in each twist and each turn. And may we accompany those we meet along the way, helping them to navigate the twists turns in their lives.

Amen

Freedom

When I was a social worker, I sometimes visited jails and secure accommodation for young people. While necessary for some people, these places were quite frightening (even for me as a visitor). I often had a feeling of being unable to breathe while there. I could feel the atmosphere of  imprisonment; of confinement. It left me anxious to get out. To be free.

As well as physical imprisonment, there are many other ways that we are kept prisoner in our lives.

Some are imprisoned in a spiral of addiction. Each day seeming impossible to get through without a drink, a smoke, a fix of gambling.

Some are imprisoned by poor self-image and esteem. We can crucify ourselves each day; telling ourselves a story of only our inadequacies.

Some are imprisoned in hopelessness. The world can feel like a cold and cruel place, with nothing to offer but pain.

Some are imprisoned by grief. The loss of a loved one can feel final and devastating. We can feel like there is no recovery from the hurt.

I have seen myself imprisoned at various times by various (seemingly powerful) prison masters. I've encountered the feeling of confinement, constriction and stagnation of my Spirit. At these times, freedom felt only like an abstract idea that applied to others and not to me.

Invariably, freedom has come and I thank God (the source) for that. Also, invariably, freedom has come after I made the same discovery time and again:
I am not in control.

Efforts to keep in control were fruitless and, in fact, kept me imprisoned. Acknowledging that I was not in control allowed me to:
Cry
Stop
Breathe
Pray
Ask for help
Once I did all of those, I was able to feel a sense of freedom. It still required that I did things for myself, though. No magic fixes here. But I found that I did things as a participant in something bigger, beyond just me. I gave up a little of my ego and found in that space there was possibility. Not as a driver, but as a passenger in life. For me, I realised that God was driving the car! And that gave me the freedom to look around and take in the sights for what they really were, rather than obsessing all the time over where the car had to go next.

May we be comforted in our times of imprisonment. May we realise that we are passengers and not always drivers in life. And may we come to experience the freedom of giving up and giving over control.
Amen

That one thing

Walking in the park today I was struck by a thought: how often I find myself in bother in life due to one particular thing. One particular approach to relationships. Particularly in family relationships. I'm quick to huff and puff and over-react. It's one thing I see in myself again and again that I don't like. I want to re-commit to letting that part of my personality go.

It reminded me of a story about Jesus meeting a rich young man. The man told Jesus that he had been a good Jewish boy. He loved his parents, went to the temple, said his prayers. What more must he do, he asked (hoping, like all of us I guess that the answer would be, 'nothing at all. You're sorted!') Jesus told him he was lacking one thing; he was to go and sell his possessions and give them to the poor. (The story ends saying that the man went away sad).

Now this could be seen as a call to radical poverty and for giving to the poor. It is that indeed. But it strikes me that Jesus saw that the young man had 'that one thing', that was holding him back. Perhaps the young man had attached too much importance to his money. Or perhaps his riches were stopping him from being all he could be in relationships with others.

What's 'that one thing' in your life? What's 'that one thing' that holds you back in re-lationship with yourself, with other, with God? It might be something that you know already but struggle with (like my example above), or it maybe you're yet to discover and acknowledge it.

Whatever it is, you can let it go. It's holding you back from being all you can be. It's limiting you in your relationships. We don't have to be like the rich young man and simply go away sad. We don't have to be afraid either. There's a profound line in the story I've spoke of. It goes like this: Jesus looked steadily at the young man and loved him. We do all of this in the context of being loved. Now. Right now. The rich young man was loved even though he ultimately didn't make the move to give away his riches and went away sad.

May we spend some time looking for 'that one thing'. May we work on letting it go. And may we know that we are loved and supported through this all.
Amen

For those who have lost touch with their own self worth

There are two battles: external and internal. Let's deal with each.
External: We are bombarded with images and media messages about what 'perfection' is. Invariably it involves a body shape, food intake regime, bank balance, house style and clothes that many of us simply don't have. Sometimes we can get caught up in that game and feel like we're missing something. Or worse, that we ourselves are falling short by not conforming to the 'ideal'. It's a game. Don't play it.

Other external forces can be at work too. In relationships (family, work and other) people can be given the message, directly and indirectly, that they are no good. Or not good enough. If we're honest with ourselves sometimes we are guilty of sending that message to others. Let's stop. Or standing back while others do the damage. Let's step in and stop them.

Internal: People can lose touch with their self worth through internal forces at work. Negative self talk, depression, mixed up thinking. And other things. When these things are at work, life can seem pretty awful. We can feel pretty awful.
So if you're in the midst of one or both of those battles (or if you know someone who is) I'd like to say this:
You are a person of great worth. At your core you are a person of dignity. A beautiful Creation with unlimited potential to live life and live it to the full. In your essence, you are goodness.

May all those who have lost touch with their own self worth reconnect to it. May we all come to realise the role we can have with so many people in making this happen.
Amen

Stop and smell the roses

My good friend Fr Tom Toner (RIP) used to say 'make sure you take time to stop and smell the roses' when other priests asked his advice. What I think he meant was that all of us would do well to recognise that life can be so busy that we get caught up in business (busyness) and miss the real point. And the point he was making is that there is beauty out there. God's beauty made real in nature and in other people.

I once read about a piece of research some scientists did. They got groups of people from young to old and blindfolded them and blocked their ears. They asked them to indicate when a minute had elapsed from their blindfolding and earplugging. What they found was that the younger people indicated early and the older indicated later. In other words older people experienced one minute going quicker than they thought. Time goes quicker as you get older. My parents used to say this to me and now I'm beginning to experience it myself!

Life can be busy and time can go by quickly. We can get caught up in (often empty) action and miss some of life's beauty: a smile from a loved one, an act of kindness, a piece of art, a song that reminding us of childhood, a lover's embrace, a moment of union with God in prayer.

May we take each day we have as a full 24 hours (86,400 seconds) of possibility. May we stop and smell the roses. Thank you Tom
Amen

The gift of the vulnerable

What a joy it is to be around those who society would tell us are 'useless' or 'past it'. Those who are vulnerable through old age or sickness often develop an honesty and genuine humility that is refreshing to be about. They also often have a really keen eye on the world. They can sift out the things that don't matter and focus on the things that do- like relationships, faith, love.

May those who are vulnerable through sickness or old age have plenty of people around them who realise how much of a gift they really are. And may we who aren't (yet) vulnerable in this way keep our eyes and ears open for the opportunity to reach out in love to the vulnerable.
Amen

Sons of the father

There was a wise old man. In his old age he found that he needed people more than he used to. Thankfully, he had two sons. Once per week or so he asked both children to do his shopping for him.

The first child often said, 'yes, that's no problem'. However, after saying 'yes' the first son rarely followed through and actually did the shopping. He meant well and when he said 'yes' he meant it in that moment. But life was busy and drew him in other directions. The wise old man knew this and when he thought about his son, he smiled and hoped he could deal with all the busyness of life.

His second son was different. When the father asked him to do some shopping, his first reaction was to see only the busyness of life and say, 'no'. Usually, however, he came back to his father a few days later after finding a space in his life and offered to do the shopping. Sometimes the father sent him and sometimes he had already found someone to do the shopping that week. On those occasions the son scolded himself and told himself that the next time he'd say 'yes' to his father. But the next week came and his first response was 'no' again. He could only see the busyness. When the father thought of him, he smiled again and hoped that his son didn't beat himself up too much.

Sometimes, however, the first son said 'yes' and followed through. And sometimes his second son fought the urge to see the busyness and actually said 'yes' first time. On those occasions the father smiled again.
I know which son (daughter) I am. Do you? The father smiles at you.
Amen

The seasons in our lives

Most of us know the song by the Byrds from the 60s called *Turn, Turn, Turn*. It tells us that there's a season for everything. There's a time live, a time to die. A time to gather, a time to throw away. It's based on scripture. Different times for different things. Life looking different at different times.

This got me thinking about looking at my life in terms of its 'seasons'. Looking back I can recognise the times of my life where the season was one of great happiness and growth (the birth of my children and their early years for example).
A season of learning about the world from an adult perspective (leaving school and going to university for example).

A season of learning about the finite nature of life (the death of my lovely granny and granda for example and many more loved ones since).

A season for growing up and learning about responsibility (buying a house, getting in and then out of debts – and then in and out again a few times!)

A season of becoming who I am (sensing a call from God to come closer and really appreciate the love available to all)

Life does indeed have seasons. Seasons with general movements in certain ways. Recognising these seasons allows me to explore the learning available. It allows me to look for and find God's hand in the general movement – even, or particularly, in the difficult seasons.

I mostly see those seasons through the rear view mirror. It's easier in hindsight. But perhaps the invitation is to look for the season in the here and now.

My white beard tells me I'm in the season of ageing. I wonder what the learning will be? I wonder where God's hand will reveal itself in this season? One thing I know, God's hand is in it. And if I can be open to viewing this season in my life as one of possibilities, I'll find the learning, the development, the growth.

What's your season of life? And what can recognising it teach you?

The employed and the unemployed

For those in employment. May we recognise the great gift it is to have a job (even if the job you have is difficult, badly paid or stressful). May we see a way to give our all in our jobs and look for meaning in them.

For those who are unemployed. People can lose more than an income when unemployed. They can lose a sense of purpose or even lose a sense of themselves. May they know that they are still a whole person. And may work come their way. Today's culture may be predominantly one of 'put effort in as long as you are getting a reward at the end'. Fair enough, we all need money to live.

But let's be counter cultural (there's a rebel in me!). We all, employed or unemployed, can find ways of working at the service of others. Maybe through volunteering or in some small acts of kindness and compassion to others.
May we all be the presence of Love and Service to those we meet.
Amen

Cycling into the wind

I was cycling one morning on a road that would be one of my regular routes in Portugal. It takes me out of Lagos and into the countryside. It's really beautiful. I cycled it two days ago and it was a real joy. But today the Algarve wind was blowing and what had seems almost easy two days ago was tough going. I was surrounded by the same beauty but had to push so hard that it passed me by. It was only when I stopped for a water break that I realised I'd travelled a long way without really seeing anything at all.

So prayers today for anyone who feels that their life at the moment is like cycling into the wind. May the wind calm and may you feel the presence of Beauty.
Amen

Living out our purpose

When I think of my friend Fr Alan McGuckian I think of a phrase: we have a God of all possibilities. The first reading at Mass one day spoke of one possibility. Jeremiah says that God tells us, 'Before I formed you in the womb I knew you'. Let's think about that for a while. If that's the case then there a few things that strike me:
1. Our relationship with God is a very intimate and personal one. We can speak to God and God will know us (the Shepherd recognises the sheep as Jesus said often) because God formed us.
2. Our existence in this world is not accidental. Rather it is ordained – ordered and meant to be.
3. Our existence has a pre ordained purpose. In other words there are things for us to do that no other person can (or is meant to) do.

So many times life can appear pointless, difficult, tedious. But contemplating the words of Jeremiah we can have the possibility of a pointed, purposeful life. If we buy that then here's another: our job is to always look for and live out our purpose. That means living in an intentional way.
So what do you intend to do (or be) that can help you live out your pre ordained purpose? I'm gonna keep my eyes open today. Who's going to join me?
Amen

In admiration of you

Yes you. You have an admirable essence! The essence of you is pure and true and good. People can see it in you. I see it in your humour. Your compassion. Your struggling. Your competence and confidence. Your vulnerability. Your emotions. Your actions. Your loveliness. Your courage. Your love of others. I admire you and tonight I'm going to adore God for making you and putting you in my path.
Amen

The hovering Spirit

I came across this line in my prayer time tonight: 'The Lord sits enthroned above the flood'.

It reminded me of the image of the Spirit 'hovering over the chaos'.
So much chaos in our world. So many are flooded by violence, war, famine, disaster. Sometimes it's not big headline news (like the atrocities happening in Palestine at the minute) that create chaos for us and leave us feeling flooded. Sometimes it's every day stuff: debt, worry, grief, poor self image, hatred, broken relationships, addiction.

When those times hit it's hard to believe that anyone is enthroned above our flood. Let alone God. Yet, I truly believe that God does just that. God is hovering over our chaos. Not creating our chaos (us humans do that to ourselves and others in the main I think) but hovering just above it. Telling us that it'll be OK. If we but only find the God way. The way of love, peace and justice.

And here's another thing. God doesn't just hover above the chaos. God joins us in our chaos and even intervenes in it. God does this in many ways but one way is through us. When we see the God in all things, in all people, we want to reach out and help/serve those we can. In this way others' worries are sorted. Others' lonely troubles are shared and halved. Others in far off lands being bombed nightly feel the love and support of aid. Politicians make wise decisions based on respecting all life- not just white, Western, young, fit life. The suicidal man walking alone along a busy road feels someone cares when the car stops and someone speaks to him. The grieving daughter knows that her daddy is at rest and looks down in love and pride at her. The man with cancer finds peace and meaning even in the face of disease.
God is hovering over the chaos. God is enthroned above the flood. Whatever flood you are experiencing tonight, I'm praying hard for you right now. May God's presence in your flood be known to you through the love and works of others.
May we find the opportunities to be God's presence in this world and bring the floods, the chaos to an end where we can.
Amen

People among us from other lands

I saw a lot of people in town today who were here visiting this fine land. Most looked very happy indeed. Some studied maps and plotted next moves. But one couple in their late 50s were obviously having a fall out. He grunted something to her. She ignored him theatrically by throwing her nose in the air and looking away. Even on holidays marriage is hard work it seems!

May all of those who have come here for a holiday, short break, business trip or whatever the case may be have a safe stay in Belfast. May their days here be sunny (we'd all benefit from that one!) and their nights full of relaxation and entertainment. May we who live here be enriched by their presence and learn culturally from them.

May the God who causes the morning to break and the night to fall all over this world look upon all of us with love and may we look upon God with wonder and awe.
Amen

Those wandering alone and unhappy

For those we meet along the way who find life too tough. For those who are at the end of their tether.

May we see in them the essence of their being (which is always good, always God) and reflect that to them. And may we meet them and engage with them in ways that show them that they are loved and lovely.
Amen

The gift of friendship

Life is a funny old thing. An old and wise priest I know said in passing to me lately, 'I didn't know what to do with time when I had so much of it'. He's old and frail now and looking directly into the end of it (here at least). It's had me thinking. What do we spend our time chasing?

It seems to me that some of us chase many things through life: money, success, status, sex, possessions. Do any of these last? Do they fulfill all we can be? Do any of these really matter? Hmm.. Answers on a postcard.

Friendship, I think, does matter. True friendship supports, challenges, hold, shapes, carries, is carried, laughs with (never at), cries with, journeys with, sticks in with all of us. In this way friends really do help us be all we can be.

So tonight I thank God for the friends I have. I grieve for the true friends I have lost. And I wait in excitement for the friends I may have in the future. Feel free to share this status with people you regard as true friends or write their names below. Or just hold them in your prayers tonight: even better.
Amen

(This prayer is inspired by a lunch with Paddy Linden and Denis Kearney who I have had as true friends since the early 1970s)

For good sight

Not specifically thinking about literal eyesight here but prayers too for those who can't see to receive the best treatment possible. I'm thinking more for us all to see things right. My eyes are often tired; sometimes cynical; even feel like they've seen it all before. They often see with goggles of fear, anger or prejudice – usually based on protecting my ego.

May we see with fresh, non-judging and loving eyes (I call them God's eyes). That way we can see the homeless woman or man as a real person with dignity and then do something to help. We can see the person from another country 'here to take our jobs' as a person doing the best they can for their family (like generations of Irish and British people have done – they say the two things you find in every country in the world are a bottle of coke and an Irish man!) and then reach out in friendship. We can see people not only as their gender, sexuality or ethnicity and then end discrimination.

We will see people like us – imperfect but loved by God anyhow.
Amen

For those who have experienced a split with a partner

Falling out, breaking up, splitting up, living separate lives. Whatever way we speak of it, it often is a sad, difficult situation where no one wins. There's can be a voice of blame inside the head. Life can be lived in a resentful or regret-filled way. This leads to unhappiness and a sense of a life unfulfilled.

May they realise that life goes on. May they ask for forgiveness if it is called for and forgive when it is asked for. May we who know them reach out in love and friendship.

Amen

Self-acceptance

So many people struggle with the image they have of themselves. Media messages about how we should look, how we should behave, what we should wear, where we should live etc... are often unhelpful and fuel a sense of being not quite good enough in a lot of people. For some it goes much deeper than that. They struggle with an internalised image of themselves as bad or ugly or worse. Sometimes they have been told that directly or indirectly.

I've spent much of my adult life with people who at times found it hard to accept themselves as anything other than broken or worthless. Yet these same people have been the best people I've met. Their beauty still shines brightly in my memory.

May all people know what it is to be Loved and accepted especially by themselves.

Amen

New beginnings

New beginnings can be times of great joy. Think of someone beginning a new dream job. Or of someone beginning a course of study. Think about someone in a new relationship.

However, new beginnings can bring us anxiety as well. By definition if we are beginning anew, the road we are about to travel will be one we won't know yet. The new job mightn't work out. The new course might be too complicated for us. The new relationship might bring heart ache as well as roses and chocolates.

I know of some people beginning a new phase in their lives right now and it strikes me that there is another layer to new beginnings. They often follow on from an ending: something has had to die to allow for this new life. New beginnings, in this way, are often hard fought to win.

I know that my experience of grieving loved ones tells me that in order for me to move on from the debilitating grief and believe that I can go on and function as a person again, that I have to be in that grief 100%. I need to allow the grief to penetrate me and to really affect me before I can begin again.

So sometimes in going through the experience of being in poor relationships we emerge stronger and wiser with a sense of our own person-hood and goodness. This, happily, makes us fitter to be in positive relationships.

Sometimes in going through the trauma of job loss we get a sense of priorities, of our own inner strength and our ability to find purpose elsewhere.

Sometimes in going through illness we rediscover the value of health and of life and of the goodness of others.

It's easier, I think, to see God in the new beginnings. It's more of a challenge for me to see God in the thing that precedes it. The thing that must end or must be endured before a new beginning is possible. And yet, I believe, God is in everything or God is in nothing. God is in the pain with me and God invites me to a new beginning.

May we come to see all difficulties as simply the preface to a new beginning. May we reach out and help those we see in that phase of things ending or things being endured. And may we embrace all new beginnings as times of endless possibility. ***Amen***

For hearts of flesh: for new spirit

It struck me that I've seen so many executions, shootings, beatings, starving children, bereft people on TV news and Internet sites in my lifetime that images that once would have been shocking (traumatising) have become somehow sanitised or distant – as if the glass in the screen and the different clothes and languages (mostly) of the people allow me to think this is happening in a galaxy far, far away.

Images in the mid 80s of famine stricken people spurred us on to Live Aid and Geldof demanding 'Give us your f*#@ing money'. Righteous anger expressed on behalf of all whose hearts bled for fellow man and woman who starved as we threw out scraps that would have given them precious life.

Now we have image overload. The same perils – war, famine, death – but the same reaction? The same shock? The same righteous anger? I don't know. And I speak about myself here primarily.

So, may I be shocked and angry and shed tears as my brothers and sisters all over the world (and here at home) experience hardship, famine, poverty, war, death. And may I have the courage not only to have a heart of flesh but also a new Spirit of action to help where I can.

Amen

Those we love and who love us

They include (in no order at all):
Brothers
Sisters
Mothers
Fathers
Cousins
Uncles
Aunts
Grandparents
Nephews
Nieces
Friends
Husbands
Wives
Priests
Ministers
Boyfriends
Girlfriends
Work colleagues
Heroes
And so many more...
There are those tonight (maybe even among us reading this) who feel unloved/unlovable. You are neither. God loves you. Yep. You. Maybe you haven't realised just how lovely you are.

Let's spend a minute bringing some people to mind that we love. Let's ask God for good things for them.

Now let's bring to mind those who love us. Let's be thankful.

Now let's resolve to let someone/people know we love them by telling them or showing them in no uncertain terms tonight or tomorrow. As Merton says, we'll be helping them see the meaning in life.

'Love is our true destiny. We do not find the true meaning of life by ourselves. We find it with others.' – Thomas Merton

Amen

Fathers

I remember hearing Ricky Tomlinson (the actor) speaking once about his father. He said that the other kids growing up in Liverpool in the 50s were afraid of their father and he could never understand because his father was a kind and gentle man. It stuck with me. I remember thinking that I wanted to be that kind of father.

Some are with us. Some are gone but not forgotten. Some are gentle and kind. Some are not. Some are biological. Some are not. Some are living at home. Some are not. Most are broken and imperfect like the rest of us. Some, like my own, are old now. Some are young and healthy. Some, like my friend Stephen are awaiting the birth of their first born. Some, like me, are amazed at how fast the years have gone and how quick their children grow.

Let's pray for all fathers to the Father- gracious and compassionate; slow to anger and rich in love – that they may grow in their love of their children and their children's children and be guides on the road of life.

Amen

Prayers for a REBOOT

Sometimes life can get infected with sorts of bugs and viruses that corrupt our hard drive functions of thoughts, emotions and actions. These viruses can manifest themselves in all sorts of ways.

They can make us feel:

Useless

Ugly

Fat

Inadequate

Powerless

Shameful
Stupid

As a result we attempt to correct the virus by:
Always wanting more things (in the hope that we will feel good about who we through feeling good about what we have)
Trying to be in control at all times
Staying away from all people (they will see how useless I am)
Numbing myself (with alcohol, drugs, sex, money, power)
Beating myself (or others) up
Being bitter
If you find yourself with any of these symptoms, here is the anti virus to install into the hard drive for a total reboot:
God loves you

Now, I'll have to unpack that for you.
Firstly, God exists (seriously, God exists).
Secondly, God is not waiting in the sky for you to screw up so that he can laugh and punish you.
Thirdly, any concept you have of guilt is far smaller than God's concept of forgiveness.
Fourthly, if life is hard at the minute, God is not doing that to you.
Fifthly, God has plans for you (and they are great!).
Sixthly, God loves YOU. Not a version of you that the world would approve of. Not a version of you that is 'better'. God loves YOU.

Begin by being IN love. All else will flow from that reboot.
Amen

For wise leadership

Many of us find it hard to accept we need leadership at times. But the reality is that wise leadership can build us as individuals and as communities. The task of leadership is not easy. It can lead to undue criticism. I've seen myself where people almost dehumanise leaders, calling them names and deriding all they say without much thought. A former lecturer of mine put it well, 'if you put your head above the parapet they cut you off below the knees!' We can cut people off below the knees; criticise them at times knowing that if we were in their position we would do no better.
But leaders need to be questioned and challenged (with love and respect) to ensure that their leadership is wise and proper. They need to be focused and available.

Ivory tower leadership is dangerous. A true servant leader will know that she or he is working in the service of those they lead. They will be interested in them and want to know them. The Shepherd will smell of the sheep if you like.

May we be generous to our leaders as they go about their duties as best they can. And may all leaders seek to be servant leaders, caring for the people they lead (and all people) and making the world a better place.
Amen

For mission; for a sense of purpose and direction

I so often wander around in a kind of aimless (albeit harmless, sort of helpful) way. However to be fully alive, fully human, we need a sense of mission. When we connect to our purpose, our gifts, our mission- then it's game on! Yet so many of us are fooled into thinking we are not at all gifted. In fact some feel useless. No! No! No!
It's exciting to know that we each have distinct gifts and therefore a distinct mission/s in life. Our job is to acknowledge our giftedness and find our mission/s.

May we love ourselves enough to accept that we are Gifted and know that we are Called. May we look for opportunities to connect our gifts to others' needs.
Amen

Shepherds

Shepherds. I don't see a lot of them here in the west of Belfast! But when I look up to the mountain above me here I see the outline of fields that have been there for centuries. I'd say there's been a fair share of shepherds, goat herds and cow herds(?) up there in their time. All of them looking out for and after their charges.

I know in my life I have people who look out for and after me. I felt that when so many of you were thinking about me on the anniversary of my friend's death. Yesterday you shepherded me through a sad day. And I felt the benefit of your thoughts and prayers. Thank you.

May we look out for opportunities to be shepherds for each other, particularly when we find others on the margins or oppressed. And may we know that we all have a Shepherd looking out for us.
Amen

For an end to division

Often things that separate us (on a micro level in relationships or on a macro level in society) are based on half truths or misunderstanding. The results of division are hurt, hate and unhappiness.

There is another Way. Unity, understanding and mutual respect for difference. May we be interested enough to explore the reasons behind the divisions in our life, relationships and society. And once explored to move beyond them to unchartered territory of limitless possibilities.
Amen

Turning the other cheek

I was scammed out of a few quid one week (the details of which I won't go into). It gave rise to real bad feeling in me. Sadly, I was filled with frustration that turned into anger and thoughts of revenge and fantasies of confronting the person (which would have been impossible anyhow). It wasn't pretty. And it didn't make me feel any better either.

So I forgive the person and pray that they will turn away from dishonest ways. But I wish them nothing but good in their life.

So many of us struggle with turning the other cheek, or simply turning away when we are wronged. We often get involved in arguments or even caught up in holding grudges and seeking revenge. This isn't good for you. Research shows that holding on to bad feeling harms your health. While turning away, forgiving and getting on with life is a good way to decrease your risk of heart attacks!
May we look at our lives tonight and for the opportunities we might have to let go of old grudges or not so old grudges. It'll be good for our physical and spiritual health.
Amen

Travellers we meet on the road

I don't know about you but I walk a lot. And when you walk a lot you see a lot. Today I was out a few times (with my dogs of course!) and saw all sorts of life. I saw:
My cousin standing at her gate with her new born daughter

My brother just back from a few days in Iceland
The man who taught me to drive (20 odd years ago. I hadn't seen him since until today)
A man who I've seen but not talked to till today. He has (had) a dog but told me today when I saw him without it that it had died.
Noel, a great guy from Larne (teacher and worker for his parish)
My buddy and guitar guru, Kev McG
The gospel reading in my tradition today tells of two travellers on a road who met Jesus, but they didn't recognise him. I guess the lesson is to see Jesus/God/good in all we see. And the story also holds a mirror up to the fact that we don't make that effort as much as we should.
I can easily see Jesus in these people above. I'm not particularly challenged in doing that. However, when walking today I also saw:
Romanian men cleaning cars while most of the world looked at them with suspicion
Children smoking and drinking cider and shouting at passersby
Young men staring me out as they passed by
People speeding in cars
Did I make the effort to see the God/good in them?
May we challenge ourselves to find our blind spots when it comes to our prejudices. And may we recognise that it is not our job to judge.
Amen

The challenges that lie ahead for all of us

Thankfully no one knows the future of our lives on earth. However we know that we will face many challenges as we travel on. Perhaps some of us are facing challenging times right now? Good news = we do not face them alone.

May we face challenges bravely when they come along always looking to better times. And may we look out for those among us who are facing challenging times and reach out a hand of Friendship and Love. For those of us who followed the amazing story of Easter and profess a belief in the teacher who conquered the ultimate challenge it's what he would want us to do: love one another.
Amen

Hope

Some days seem tough, empty, never ending. Those days can bring suffering, bitterness, loss of hope. But there's always tomorrow.

Tomorrow can bring joy, peace, an end to suffering. That's if we believe that there can be a tomorrow. And if we believe that there is a point to all of this- to life itself. I choose to believe. I choose to hold on to a reason behind everything (and that I am small enough not to need to know the reason all the time). I choose to believe in one Greater than me. And I know that tomorrow can bring a new dawn even to those in the midst of terrible suffering.

Amen

For women. Nuff said!

Thank God for women. They bring life to our world in so many ways. Literally through childbirth, and through their wisdom, strength, energy, patience and Love. Yet in so many ways and in so many places women are discriminated against and persecuted. May women be free to fulfill their true potential. And may us men who benefit from their gifts be truly thankful for them.

Amen

For a work/life balance

When we die and go up (here's hoping) and St Peter greets us and asks us 'any regrets?' not many will reply, 'I wish I'd spent more time in work'. Instead, we might think we wish we'd spent more time:
with family
with friends
praying
reading
laughing
remembering what it's all about
helping
dancing
singing
loving
The Good News is that if you're reading this right now, you've still time to get the balance back.

Amen

In thanksgiving for mistakes

We often feel sorry for the things we have done wrong in our lives. This is right and proper and it is also right to ask for forgiveness when we need to. But mistakes are also a blessing to us if we can learn from them. They give us insight into where we need to develop ourselves in our relationship with others, with ourselves and with God.

Each mistake can open up a whole world of growth if we can move beyond feelings of guilt, shame or fear. Often the act of forgiveness and Reconciliation can help us here.

So for those of us who have made (and will continue to make) mistakes let's pray in thanksgiving for the opportunities for growth they provide. For those of you who haven't made mistakes... Look again
Amen

You

For the person you are. Not necessarily the person others see. Not the person others want you to be. But you- the person you are right now and the person you can be in the future.

You are inherently good. You are special. You are gifted. Even if you don't see or feel it. You are. Sure you have some rough edges but those can be smoothed! And besides smoothing those rough edges is part of what life's journey is about.

Do three things:
1. Believe this
2. Do something for yourself to celebrate this (something gentle and life giving)
3. Do something for others motivated by peace, love or justice (I choose to call this God)
Amen

A positive perspective

Prayers tonight for those who approach life from a 'yes' perspective. Who say yes to helping others (helping us). Who say yes to a life lived for others much more than for the self.

Saying yes is a powerful thing. Think of the people in your life who have said yes to you. In supporting you. In helping you out. In rescuing you from some difficult situation. In being your partner for life perhaps (thanks Nuala Deeds!)

It's difficult for us to say yes sometimes. It's easier to approach life from a 'no' perspective. It's safer. It less risky. It expends less energy.

Yet all good comes from a 'yes' approach. A can do approach.

In our tradition today we recognise Mary's yes. She said yes and only asked 'how will this be done?'. No preconditions. No worries. No bargaining. No self indulgence.
Amen

For anyone with money worries

Having unmanageable debt can feel like not being able to breathe. It can lead to all sorts of feelings of anxiety, worry and shame. It is often a feeling of being trapped. May all who have money worries find a Way through them. May those of us who can help offer that help when we see the need. May we support the many great organisations that reach out to those in debt. And may we together create the type of society where we eradicate debt entirely.
Amen

The good people we meet along our journeys

It's easy to fall into a trap of cynicism; thinking and/or saying that most people are greedy or dishonest or uncaring. But that's not the truth as I experience it. Most people are doing the best they can with what life throws at them. And more than that, a lot of the people we meet or know are really a great gift to us and the world. I am blessed to know so many good people. You, for example.

May we recognise, value and celebrate the good in others and try to show some of that goodness to all we meet along the way.
Amen

Hands

I've been using my hands in new ways recently, making guitars. It's been an interesting and life giving experience. And it got me thinking today about how we use our hands.

The same hands that point out others' faults can point to their beauty

The same hands that turn on the remote control for the TV (to watch the same rubbish again and again) can open a book revealing knowledge, beauty and joy

The same hands that push people away can reach out and draw them near

The same hands that destroy can create

The same hands that reach out for junk food can cook healthy food

The same hands that give the finger/s can 'speak' sign language

The same hands that shoot guns can play piano

The same hands that sign for yet another credit card can sign petitions for peace and justice

The same hands that become fists can be opened and offered in love

And thank God the same hands that so often can do useless or damaging things can build guitars.

Take a moment and look at your hands. They are instruments for good. They are your soul's tools. Let's use them wisely.
Amen

Giving up

Many times in my life I've walked (and still walk) round with hatred, anxiety, worry, hurt, pride. These have never (and I mean never, once) helped me or another person achieve anything. In fact, they have dragged me down paths I should not have gone:

Paths of self pity
Paths of broken relationship
Paths of self destructive behaviour
Paths of self righteousness
Paths of depression
Paths of fear

These paths have all had one thing in common: they lacked a sense of giving up. Giving up on:

Self reliance
The need for control
The need for certainty
Material possessions
So I pray that I can give up – the right things
Amen

For keeping on keeping on

Life can have its ups and downs for all of us. I pray that you are in one of the ups. Life's downs can come as challenges. As illness. As tensions in relationships. In disappointments. In hopes dashed. In worries.
Tonight, if you find yourself in a down time, reflect on this: we are to have life and have it to the full. There will be better times head. You are known and you are loved. If you already know, believe and feel this then maybe you could look out for someone who doesn't as yet. And when you find them, tell them to keep on keeping on.
And may the God of all consolation hold you in God's loving arms this night my friends.
Amen

The death of ego

It is with sadness that we announce the death of ego. Ego has been a close companion for many, many years.

In times of trial, ego told us the discomfort was a bad thing. We believed ego and we did what we could to get away from the trials without any real learning. This often involved denying any responsibility for the trials we found ourselves in.

In times of comfort ego told us that we needed more to be happy. As a result, we never really enjoyed comfortable moments as we sought more and more pleasure. When faced with the hardships of others, ego told us that as long as 'I'm alright Jack', all would be well. As a result we often saw the pain of others as a mild irritant and somebody else's responsibility.

Ego often demanded most of our time and we lost touch with our souls, our hearts, our desire to know God and others.

Ego kept us more interested in what we had and how we looked than how we WERE Ego wanted us to accumulate 'victories' no matter what the cost.
Ego always wanted first place. Second place is for losers, ego said.
Ego tried to smother our real and pure self.

It is with real hope tonight that we pray for the death of ego.
Amen

Moments of serenity

In your life I pray for moments when:
voices of doubt and self-doubt are quiet
affirming voices are strong
the arm stretching out for help is met by a firm grip from others
the pain subsides
mist clears
right paths are well lit
wrong paths have danger signs
we realise that those who have died are still close by
the heart is connected more than the head
quiet time is abundant
the embrace of a loved one is never far away

I pray for these moments and more in your life and mine. When they occur, may we recognise them for the gift that they are, be thankful, and accept whatever comes next on the journey.

Amen

Losing weight

I'm going to lose weight and do more exercise. I'm going to lose:

2 pounds of judging others
1 pound of sadness
3 pounds of anger
2 pounds of hopelessness
1 pound of gossip
4 pounds of hypocrisy
2 pounds of apathy

That'll make me feel lighter! To accompany my new lightness, I'll do the following exercises:

Smile more
Hug more
Kiss more
Sing more
Pray more
Reach out for help more
Listen more
Support more
Serve more

I'll feel brand new. Anyone gonna join me in my new fitness regime?

Amen

For proper order

There are those now last who will be first, and those first who will be last. What could that mean?
Who is first to be blamed for things?
Who is first to be hurt by budget cuts?
Who is first to do all the chores round the house?

Who is first to feel pain and hurt?
Maybe those people could do with a break and be further down that particular pecking order.
Who is last to be comforted?
Who is last to see justice?
Who is last to get relief from pain and hurt?
Who is last to be built up, affirmed and encouraged?
Who is last to get a hug or a kiss?
Who is last to feel like a 'somebody'?
Maybe those people could be first in the queue for a change.
Who today could you make a 'first'?
And where could you make a sacrifice and become a 'last'?
We can make these things live amongst us.
Amen

The people and situations that are dear to you

As each of us go about our lives right now – some going to bed, some too worried to sleep, some on the other side of the world and still experiencing daytime, some working, some nursing sick relatives, some praying Night Prayer, some talking to friends and family- we each have people and situations on our mind.
These things are those which concern us. They occupy space in our minds and hearts and souls.

So right now as you read this, unite yourself with the others who are doing the same.

Call to mind those things that concern you. Unite them with the concerns of others. Pray for the resolution of the situations and the development of the people you care about and those that others care about.

Now let go and accept the outcome. Be at peace and pray that others are at peace too.

Pray for all that prospers you.
Amen

Those who are afraid

Fear can be a powerful thing in our lives...If we give it the energy it needs to affect us. It can lift us out of reality and tell us all sorts of stories about how awful future events are going to be. I can speak with some authority on this as fear comes to visit in my life sometimes. I'll tell you about one time.

I used to be afraid of flying. I used to panic for about a week before the flight. I then sat almost rigid with fear during the flight. My relief after landing was only brief, because I almost immediately began to be afraid for the next time I was going to have to fly. Eventually I gave up and stopped flying. For about 5 or 6 years.
My fear was not based on any personal experiences of danger on a plane. It wasn't based on statistics (we know that driving is more dangerous and yet I drove all through that time). It was irrational and damaging to me. I put myself through all sorts of unnecessary stress and worry. And stopping flying limited my life experiences. And yet it continued for quite some time.

I wish I could go back to that time and take myself aside for a quiet word. I'd say, 'be not afraid' (one of the most common things Jesus said). I'd tell myself not to get caught up in 'what if' and worst case scenarios that weren't going to happen anyhow.

Eventually I overcame my fear of flying. I did it with a mix of prayer and meditation and then self talk (that came from the first two). It worked for me. Why not give it a go?

So tonight I want to say to myself and to anyone who is in a time of fear: 'be not afraid'. Your fear can only affect you if you give it energy. Don't. Realise that it is only a story with an ending that is yet to be written.

May we who fear, 'be not afraid'. May we reach out to those we see in fear and comfort them. And may we come to know the Consolation of the One who holds us in our times of fear and walks with us to times of peace.
Amen

Thanksgiving

I live in a house
I am warm
I had a nice dinner
I can walk
I have a job (the best job in the world)
I have a wife (also the best in the world!)
I have a family
I have friends
I am not in immediate danger of death (as far as I know)
I have more guitars than I need
I have dogs who love me at my feet
I drive a car
God is love

There are many things wrong in the world. I cannot hope to make a difference in that world until I recognise how much I have to be thankful for. In that space I am much more able to see things as they are.

May we acknowledge that in amongst our difficulties there are also some things to be thankful for. May we seek to be someone that somebody else is thankful for. May we always give thanks where it is due. And may we grow in our thanks to and for the God who does nothing but look steadily at us and love us.
Amen

Being in the dark

There are many areas of my life where I feel a bit 'in the dark'. That is to say, in that place where I have little or no control; I don't have all, or maybe even a lot, of the information I would like to have; I see no ways to go.

Traditionally I have feared being in the dark. I have reacted against it and tried to 'get into the light' any which way I can. That has sometimes led to me making rash decisions that have not been the best to say the least.

And yet, the dark can be seen in other ways.

For example, the place of no control is a place where we can let go of the pretence that there is any control to begin with. I believe we are part of a bigger picture that can never and should never be under my control (I wouldn't really know what to do with it!).

Acknowledging that I am in the dark will allow me to see that in the dark there are bits and pieces of the information I need floating around- in the shape of other people, of insights from prayer for example.

Acknowledging that I can see no way of my own that I can go, allows me to consider that others may hold the key to the right path for me.

Only by truly being in the dark can I begin to reach out to others and to reach out for God. The dark can be a scary place. It can be a place of anxiety. However, it can also be a place of transformation; a place of good decision making; a place to recognise my needs.

The irony of course is that it is only by knowing what darkness is, that we can truly know what light is.

May we never be afraid of the dark. May we let go of our need to be in control. May we acknowledge our need of others when we are in the dark. And may we recognise that we can always reach out in the dark and find One who can lead us to the light. *Amen*

Inspiration

At times life can be tough. We can be swamped by bad news, ill health, fractious relationships, worries and trouble. I'm struck by how our language at these times often refers to 'air' and 'breath'. We can feel that the 'air has been taken out of our sails'. Our bodies sometimes hold our worries and we can feel that breathing itself is difficult. We can hear ourselves speak of the need of 'breathing space' away from our troubles.

Reflecting on this recently I found that in my times of trial I often feel the need for 'inspiration'. And then I found the real definition of the word 'inspire':
Inspire – to breathe or blow into; to impart an idea or truth.

Turns out we were right all along. We do need 'air' and 'breathing space'! In the Christian tradition we associate air, wind and breath with the Holy Spirit – this is what we call the person in the Trinity that activates, motivates, creates, opens the way. The Spirit breathes life into us and helps us to move along the path of life.

So, if you find yourself tonight in a time of trial, trouble or worry, just take a moment to breathe. Breathe deeply. And as you do so, consider the possibility that you breathe in more than air; you could be breathing in the Spirit that truly inspires us. Give it a go, even if you have difficulty with the language of faith. Breathing deeply is good for you!

May the Spirit of God fill you, energise you, prosper and protect you.
Amen

The big picture

I was talking to someone today who told me that as a young person they projected hate onto others. But now they could see the big picture they had given up hate completely. I was struck by this person's honesty and journey from hatred. What had they seen in the big picture, I wondered? I didn't get a chance to ask. It must have been a great thing or things.

That got me thinking about my big picture. What is in my big picture – a picture that could help me journey from unhelpful thoughts, feelings and actions towards more loving ones. So I closed my eyes and tried to see that big picture.

Trees, flowers and grass
Wide open spaces
But filled with people
Friend and foe alike
All with something to teach me
And with beauty at their core
Family standing closest
Embracing me
Hurt laid bare as unnecessary
Love held up as all
Bonds of connection
Binding us together

Eyes towards the good
Eyes towards God

That's the big picture that could help me travel well in life. It's also, ironically, the picture I struggle most to see. I mainly get caught up in narrow, unhelpful pictures that take me further from Love.

May we all close our eyes and see our own big picture. May we focus on that picture rather than the small, unhelpful pictures life can throw at us. And may we all know the support of God in our travels from hatred towards love.
Amen

Walking in sync

Every day I walk with my dog. It's a daily routine. I've accepted it happily as part of my life.

Today as I walked along, I realised that we were in sync. The walk felt effortless. The pressure that there sometimes is wasn't there. It felt right. No longer were there two walking. It was more like a Jim-dog unit walking together.

Walking out of sync with dog usually happens when I don't pay attention to the walk. Sometimes I lag behind, my pace too slow. Sometimes I walk ahead, the pace too fast.

And yet, I've come to trust God and know that if we're in sync the walk will be better. Not only that, but I'll be able to walk further and see more along the way. My mind will be clearer – less concerned with getting back in sync, more concerned for the journey and those I meet along the way.

Every day I walk with God. I pray to be ever more in sync.
Amen

For the seeds we plant

I remember in primary school that we planted seeds in a yoghurt pot. We pushed them deep down into the pot and watched. Every day we watered them and watched. And slowly but surely (out of sight) the seed shot out roots. The roots took hold in the soil and the plant grew. The type and colour of the plant grew according to the type of seed that was planted. It was a great activity but one that has not led to me being any good around the garden!

I continue to plant seeds, though. I plant seeds every day in my interactions with others. In the words I say and in the actions I take. Just as surely as in my primary school yoghurt pot, the seeds I plant now shoot out roots in those I interact with. Out of sight and mainly unknown to me those roots take hold in others.

I wonder what type of seeds I plant? What type of flower or plant will result? Will it be a beautiful rose that builds the person's confidence and allows them to know a wonderful world full of goodness (I call that God)? Or will it be a thorn bush that will choke the person's self esteem and allow them to see only a world of pain, hurt and hopelessness?

May we know that our actions and words impact on others. May we seek to plant seeds of hope and goodness. And may we acknowledge that while we plant the seeds, we aren't in charge of the garden!
Amen

Turbulence

I was in Glasgow one day. I flew out early in the morning (red-eyed due to the early start), and flew back in that night (red-eyed from a long day's work). I really enjoyed being a stranger in a strange land. The unfamiliar accents, the different coloured faces, the different styles of dress that I heard and saw gave me a sense of newness: a sense of possibility.

On the way home, as we neared our landing, we experienced turbulence. The air plane rocked side to side, as if skidding on some mid-air invisible ice track. It bumped up and down.

A young person near me who was travelling alone held her arms out, palms pressed tightly against the back of the seat in front of her. The man in front of me popped open a rogue tin of beer (the cabin crew had cleared away all glasses etc. and had asked us to put everything away) and he held tight to that! A mother and daughter beside me reached out and held each others' hands. Again they held tight. It struck me that in times of turbulence in our lives we instinctively reach out for something to hold tight to.

At times, we reach out and hold tight to things that ultimately do us no good (like the man in front of me perhaps?). Other times we reach out and feel there's no one there (like the young person who held onto the seat).

And yet other times we reach out and find the Presence. The presence of someone who can hold us in our turbulent times (like the mother and daughter who found each other tonight).

And when the turbulence ended tonight we were all a little glad; all a little more appreciative of the times when there was no turbulence. I wonder if we'll sustain that thankfulness? Or if we'll simply forget the blessing of coming through the turbulence- until the next time and we get a chance to re-learn the lesson and to reach out once more?

May we appreciate the times in life when turbulence is far away. May we live through the turbulent times, learning from the experience. And may we all come to know that when we reach out, there is always someone Present.
Amen

Redemption

Redemption: the action of regaining or gaining possession of something in exchange for payment, or clearing a debt.

The definition above speaks of two elements to the story of redemption. Firstly, it speaks of the (re)gaining of something. Secondly, it speaks of the payment that redeemed or won or bought that thing.

But I think there are three parts to the story. I'll set them out here:

Firstly, there is the loss. Or the pain. Or the straying from the correct path. Or the hurting of others. Or the turning the back to God. Redemption cannot take place without this part. There would be nothing to redeem if that was so. Therefore, mistakes, sins, errors, painful moments, mess ups (call them what you will) are not only an inevitable part of everyone's life. I believe they are a necessary part. They are part of our great story of living life long enough to really grow up. Now does that mean we go about trying to mess up? Of course not. That's not being grown up either. However, accepting the falls as inevitable and being open to learn from them-that is part of growing up.

Secondly, there is the payment. This is an interesting part. Because...It's free! Yep, redemption is freely given. When we look back to Jesus in the scriptures we see that he just throws healing, forgiveness, redemption, new beginnings, freedom all around the place. He gives it to men, women, children, foreigners, the in crowd, the out crowd (particularly the out crowd), Jews, Samaritans, lepers, crippled people, even dead people. Free redemption for all. Nobody less or more worthy of redemption than others. No bargains to be made. No contracts to be signed. There's nothing we can do to buy redemption. (Or so it seems. But I'll come back to that in a moment).

Thirdly, there is the thing that is redeemed. And that thing is us. Ourselves. Our real and true selves. We can discover who we really are. We can live a truly adult life (lots of us grow older but don't necessarily grow up). We can see ourselves, others and the world for what they all truly are: works of God.

And how does this happen? It happens when we really know God. When we really experience God. Not only in our heads. But in our very beings.We often really experience God in the difficult times of life: when we are sick, when those we love are sick, when we have really messed things up, when we feel lost. That's why I think making mistakes, pain, loss, grief, sinning are a necessary part of life. It's there that we learn to let go of ourselves and reach out to others and to God.

Now to get back to the point about whether redemption is free or not. When we really encounter God, we change. We grow. We grow up. And when we do this, we do other things. We pray more. We see the opportunities to help others more. We treat others as we would like to be treated. We set ourselves aside more. These could be construed as the price of redemption. But I see them as the fruits or rewards or outcomes of redemption. No amount of bargaining with God can 'win' us redemption. It's free- when we come to know it's free and come to know God.

Redemption is not just some remote or exclusive word. It is the stuff of real life. Just as knowing God is not just some academic or hypothetical scenario. It is the stuff of really living. We find redemption in God and God in everything.
Amen

The Readybrek glow and the all day breakfast

Growing up in the cold and dark ages of the 1970s there was a breakfast product that we used to eat called Readybrek. It was a kind of porridge. It was a really thick and filling breakfast.

The advertisers told us that it set us up for the day and that it gave us the 'Readybrek glow' like in the photo. They told us that we would have the warm glow all day and that our days would be much better for it. They showed us pictures of the poor souls who didn't eat Readybrek. They travelled throughout life without the glow. I ate Readybrek and often imagined that I felt the heat of the glow as I went out to school.

Now that I'm older I don't eat Readybrek. Too many times I start the day badly and definitely feel anything but 'glowing'. I start the day tired and in bad form some days. I start some days feeling hopeless for the day ahead. I start other days ready to argue or fight with... well whoever is going to get in my way. I need to learn how to start the day with something or things that will give me a 'glow' for the day ahead. What might they be?

I could start the day:
Spending five more minutes in prayer than I usually do
Naming five things that I can be thankful for
Naming three things that I am going to ask for help with
Eating a sensible and healthy breakfast
Being honest with myself about my life
Calling to mind the relationships I need to work on
Naming three things I can do to work on the relationships above
Thinking about those in my community who are less well off than they need to be
Naming one thing I can do to change that situation
Looking in the mirror and, no matter what I think I see, telling myself that I am unique and gifted and have a purpose

I can almost feel the 'Readybrek glow' coming on! And these don't have to be things I only do at the start of my day. They can be a kind of 'all day breakfast'. I can choose stop off points through the day and revisit this list (and add to it). That way I can have the glow throughout the day.

May we all have the feeling of 'glowing' throughout our day. May we all know that we are unique and have a purpose in life. May we greet the world head on each day with a sense of possibility. May we remember and work to help those who literally have no food to break their fast in the mornings. And may God bless us all this night.

Amen

The Source

I was talking to an orthopaedic specialist today who was telling me something very interesting about pain. She told me that someone could have pain in their foot and the source of that pain is not actually in their foot, but in the nerves of their spine (anyone who has had sciatica will know this I'd say). She said that the pain in the foot is known as 'referred pain'. To treat the foot in this case would be of no use. It would be important to return to the source. Wow! That has been with me all day today. It seemed to resonate with me on a deep level.

There are often things in my life that cause me pain or discomfort or annoyance. For example, I meet with people and situations that get on my nerves. People who are the cause of me feeling really mad. Situations that are the cause of great stress.Or are they? Maybe I need to go back to the real source of my annoyance. I would say that a lot of the time the real source of my annoyance lies with my own shortcomings: my attachment to my pride or my ego; my inability to see things from someone else's point of view; my unwillingness to change or develop or grow.
The source of the things that make us uncomfortable can lie in our past- in things we have not dealt with or resolved- rather than the things presently in front of us. In these situations we often try to treat the discomfort, pain or annoyance as we see it. This rarely works long term- because it's referred pain and we have not gone back to treat the referral source. Going back to the referral source may be more painful in the short term. But it is also the way to tap into possibility for true healing.

Another idea occurred to me throughout the day as well. It was around the word: source. It struck me that to return to the source is also a great way to describe our journey in getting to know God. God is the source of all life and of all possibility. And God accompanies and strengthens us in our efforts to deal with the referral source of our pain and discomfort in life.

May we see the real source of our pain and discomfort in life- not just the referred pain. May we have the courage to face the real source of our pain. And may the God who is the Source of all life fill you with hope, strength and joy.

Amen

Being on edge

I was reminded in a conversation that I have always had a tension in my life between being mainstream and being on the margin. I have an interesting relationship with authority. I like acceptance and that draws me to the centre of things and to work with those in authority (even, at times, becoming one in authority). I also am naturally a bit subversive and dislike rules. This combination of traits probably explains why I am a church worker with a million tattoos!

There are a couple of dangers I need to look out for. I offer them here wondering if they might speak to you in your life.

My desire to be accepted and to work with and for those in authority can sometimes keep me all 'in the head' – working from intellect only. This, in turn, can mean that I run the risk of being blinded to individuals and to those who speak from outside the mainstream. I can run the risk of colluding with a culture of bureaucracy and legality. And run the risk of always looking for certainty and security.

My subversive, individualistic bent can keep me all 'in the heart and gut' – working from instinct and intuition only. This, in turn, can leave me open to going against perceived wisdom and authority simply because it is coming from authority. I can over identify with those who are also naturally subversive and collude in their efforts to 'bring the system down' – even when the system isn't that bad. I can seek comfort in (creating) chaos and uncertainty.
Boy! I'm a mixed up kid.

What I have found in my journey of getting to know my self is that I do best on the edges of both of these big positions. When I can have a healthy respect for authority and systems, maintaining the ability to be curious and ask questions- questions motivated by a genuine desire for things be better.

And I do best when I stay on the edges of those positions through prayer, silence and meditation (for me, meditation on the person of Jesus – human and divine).
I wonder where your position in life is? Where do you do best? And what helps you maintain your best position in life?

May we all grow in our relationship with our selves. May we encounter wisdom, healing and strength in the invitation to know Jesus. And may our paths cross on the great journey of life.
See you on the edges! *Amen*

The Tufty Club (bear with me)

For those people of a certain age you may remember the
Tufty Club. For those of you who don't, let me explain.

I grew up in the 70s. There were a variety of public awareness and public safety campaigns that we were invited to
take part in. For example, do you remember 'cycling profi-
ciency'? Lessons to ensure that you could ride your bike well
and safely. Class stuff from an altogether more innocent
seeming time.

Well another of those campaigns involved the Tufty Club. Tufty, God bless him, was
a red squirrel who wore human clothes and wanted all the boys and girls to be safe
on the roads.

He had a catchphrase: Stop, look, listen. It was drummed into us in school and at
home. We knew it when we left the house.
When we had to cross the road, the catchphrase inevitably came to mind and we did
what it told us. It was genius really. And it no doubt saved lives.

Well, in homage to the 70s I'm inviting you to join the Tufty Club tonight. I'm inviting you to: Stop. Look. Listen.

Stop: Each day, find time to stop. To go to a quiet place by yourself and simply be.
The busyness of life can become a drug. We can be addicted to noise and bustle. We
can tell ourselves that it's the only way to be; that it's the nature of life in modern
times. But that's a story. It's important to take time to stop. How else are you going
to look and listen?

Look: See the world around you for what it is. See the beauty of simple things. See
flowers and animals and art and buildings and people. Look at your life with honest
eyes. Not with rose tinted glasses that tell you everything is fine when it's not. But
not with eyes that tell you that there is no hope and that everything is awful either.
Look at yourself and see your real self. See the child that you were and are. See the
beauty of you at your core. Be thankful. You're now ready to listen.

Listen: We need quiet to listen. Practise not talking. Allow quietness to fall on you.
Still yourself. This will take time. So, practice each day. Spend time by yourself.

Pray. Read scripture or a book that gives wisdom. In the quietness, listen to what you hear. They say God speaks in the silence.

May we all take time to stop, look and listen. May we hear God when we do. May all children be safe on the roads. And may the God of all consolation bless you and your families this night.
Amen

In remembrance

The world has been gripped by two conflicts so huge, so all encompassing that they were called 'World Wars'. The world, currently, is blighted by war in many, many regions. So much so that it feels like another World War in ways. We here in Ireland have been no stranger to these world wars. No bystander. And we also have our own internal war/s that have brought misery and death over the years.

2014 was the 100th year since the beginning of the First World War. And so I pray specially for the millions of people (including members of my family) who fought and/or died in that war. It's interesting how we remember these things. We call that war the 'great' war. And yet it brought death and destruction on a scale not seen in the world before. We learned how to industrialise war, death and mutilation. We built machines and weapons so horrible that we banned them almost straight away. But the genie was out of that particular bottle. We continue to use our God given intellect to design ever more efficient ways to kill our sisters and brothers.

It was called 'the war to end all wars'. It didn't. It sowed the seeds for another world war. But saying that a war could end wars doesn't make sense. It's a bit like saying 'here's an alcoholic drink that will end alcoholism' or 'here's a drug that will end our need for drugs'. The First World War did not and could not end all wars.
Only peace, love and justice can end all wars.

And in my prayer of remembrance, I'm really praying for that. For the memory of the dead and for peace, love and justice. For those who fought and for peace, love and justice. For those who lost loved ones and for peace, love and justice. For peace. For love. For justice.

May God bless us all today. May we stand as one in remembrance of all peoples killed in all wars. And may we work for peace in our hearts, our families, our communities, the world.
Amen

Home

There are many places and situations where I get that 'I'm home' feeling. You know that feeling where you feel, secure; in the right place; that things are as they should be; that you are able to be who you really are. These are some of them for me (in no particular order):

St Meryl Park
Rossnowlagh
Praying with Scripture
St. Teresa's Church
Kissing Nuala
Hugging my children
Being with my parents, brothers and sisters
Talking to Alan
Falls Park
Talking to my cousins
Playing guitar with Kevin
Playing snooker with Boylers
Writing
Praying at my office
Spending time with Denis and Paddy
Singing
Knock
Laughing with Michele
Igreja Santa Maria, Lagos
Praying at my kitchen table
Petting my dogs
Family parties

I pray that you have places and situations to put on your 'I'm home' list too. I pray for those who have no home- physical or otherwise. I pray that I may strive to make others feel 'at home'.
Amen

Pay back

I had occasion to spend an afternoon in the emergency department of a local hospital this afternoon. In amongst the ill and injured people I saw a man I know well.

(Bear with me here as I won't name this man to respect his privacy.) He was not ill himself. Rather he was accompanying a friend who was ill. The ill man was a man in his 60s. He was drunk- I mean drunk. Incoherent, vomiting, sliding off the seat drunk. People stared at him. Their stares were heavy with judgement, even disgust. After a while, the man I knew saw me and came over to talk (his friend was having a snore-filled nap at this stage). I asked him about his friend. He told me that his friend was an alcoholic who had been sober for a year, but then fell off the wagon at a family funeral a couple of weeks ago. He had been well and truly off the wagon and off his head since. Today, he began to bleed from various exits on his body. Unpleasant and frightening stuff. He did all he could – he reached out to his friend; the man I know. And so, he took his friend to hospital. He sat with him. He sat through the slurred words, the vomit, the disapproving stares of others. And he did it with a sense of practical love and even a sense of joy. I told him that I thought what he was doing was great.

He looked at me and said: 'No. It's payback'.
I knew what he meant. The man I know is an alcoholic as well. He had met the ill man while they were in rehab together. They had rooms beside each other. They had shared their stories and their journey to sobriety together.
I knew that the payback he spoke of was the paying back of friendship and time shared together. But I knew it was more. It was pay back for all of the things the man I knew had done while still drunk. Pay back for the bad times by contributing to the healing of another.

When I left the hospital, the man I knew was just arriving back after having gone to his friend's house to collect his pyjamas etc.. for his stay in hospital. He would, he told me, be there for his friend when he got out. And he would help him back on to the wagon.

The man I know is a hero. I am proud to know him.

May we look to the times when we did wrong. May we seek forgiveness. And may we look to pay back for our own wrongdoings.
Amen

Silence

It can be a noisy old world can't it? Sometimes that noise can be good noise: music, laughter, debate, wise words, loving comments.

Sometimes that noise can be not so good or even harmful: scorn, ridicule, name calling, put downs. Then there's the noise of the world we live in: calls to buy buy buy; calls to war war war; calls to look out for me me me.

We also have noise inside ourselves. Our relationship with ourselves can be a fraught one at times. Some of us have an internal dialogue that isn't always healthy for us or for those around us.

So tonight I'm praying that we all take some time in silence. We could start tonight. We could put the tablet/phone/laptop down. We could turn the TV/radio/iPlayer off. We could... be.

In the silence, so much can happen. We can relax. We can centre ourselves. We can become aware of what's going on for us. They say in the silence God speaks. So often we listen to other voices. Maybe tonight we can listen out for God's voice. Even if you don't believe in God, why not spend some time in silence and listen. Maybe you'll be surprised!

May we take a break from all the noise around us. May we listen for a Voice other than our own. And may God bless and protect you and your loved ones this day. ***Amen***

Finding the right way to walk the path together

So many times in life it can seem that people are walking different paths; separated by belief systems and approaches to living.

And yet there is only one path – living life itself. Of course, we can choose differing ways to walk that path (and if we're honest we'll recognise that we don't always walk that path well).

But if we walk the path as well as we can, and meet others on the way acknowledging that they, too, are walking as well as they can, then we can find ways to walk the path together. And in doing so, we can hold on to beliefs and traditions as well as holding others in love and compassion. Others who differ from us.

So that is my prayer. May I walk the path as well as I can (for me that means walking as close to God and the teachings of Jesus and the Church as I can). And may I always meet others as fellow travellers worthy of my respect, love and compassion no matter how they choose to walk the path. Doing this, I might even learn something along the way!
Amen

The old and gnarly

I took this picture in the City Cemetery in Belfast some time ago. It was a cold and dark morning and I saw the old, gnarled piece of wood sitting there. It struck me as having a certain sensibility and dignity – despite and because of its age. I stared at it for a few minutes and my mind wandered and wondered. I found myself contemplating the nature of God. I settled on the image of God as the 'vine' and us as branches. Because I don't live in a coun-try where we grow grapes I didn't realise for a long time what a vine looked like – the old gnarled trunk that aged in the ground over many decades. It lays down firm roots and each year shoots out vibrant, fruit-filled branches. Once the branches have borne their fruit and lived their lives, they are cut away. The vine remains. Most people see the branches and the fruit. Not the old, wise vine. And yet the branches would not exist without the vine. Lovely!

The image of the branches too strikes me as meaningful. Each branch connected to the vine. And therefore to each other through the vine. Maybe the outer edges of the branches do not contemplate the vine. They may not even know or believe it exists. Being a branch may seem all there is. And yet, the vine is there. Caring for and growing those branches as much as the branches closer to the vine and knowing of its existence. No hierarchies for the vine. Just branches to grow (love).

Take a minute and dwell with this image. God as an old, wise vine deeply rooted. Pulsing with an energy that God transmits to us – life itself. God who wants us to thrive, grow and be fruitful. The vine connected intimately to its branches.

If you don't have an image of God or perhaps if you find it difficult to believe there is a God, maybe this image will touch you as deeply as coming upon that old piece of wood in the cemetery touched me. I invite you to let it do so.

May we come to know the Vine. May we seek to bear fruit that lasts in our lives. And may God bless you, your family and your loved ones this night my sister and brother branches!
Amen

Standing radically in peace

In so many ways in our world we are faced with situations that seem to demand that we stand in one 'camp' or another in 'defence' or in 'opposition'; to 'fight our corner' or 'protect' a tradition or belief. Now, I'm not saying that there is nothing worth standing for or believing in.

However, I am hearing and seeing the language of warfare all around. And I do not stand for or believe in warfare. I choose to stand radically for peace. I stand for forgiveness, understanding, unity, love. And I do so inspired by my faith in God and my developing relationship with Jesus. That is my way of walking the path. I respect yours.

Battle lines drawn in the sand (even on dearly held beliefs) will end in violence, misery and hurt. And that is not the Way.
May we explore the nature of our existence and come to an understanding of our purpose in life. May we live according to our beliefs. May we seek to draw each other into a deeper understanding of love and peace (I call that God). And may the God of all wisdom enlighten our little minds as we journey (for a relatively short time) through life.
Amen

Weathering the storm

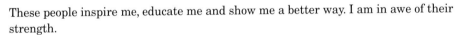

Look at this picture. It's a tree on a mountain top. In winter. After heavy snow. In strong wind. And it keeps going. It bears up and goes on. I am struck by the strength of the thing.

It reminds me of people I am blessed to know in my life who exhibit great strength.

I'll not name anyone but I know people who:
have overcome childhood trauma and have grown up to be beautiful, strong and selfless
fight illness and pain with a resolve I don't possess
are beating addiction and helping others in the process
hold others in love, even in the face of prejudice and judgement
give the gift of their lives for others

These people inspire me, educate me and show me a better way. I am in awe of their strength.
Amen

For pausing

I've learned (and then relearned) the benefits of pausing. Of taking a moment in silence (in my case, silent prayer) in the midst of dilemmas, negotiations, problems. It gives me a better sense of perspective. And it allows me to sort through what is my own' stuff', prejudice and bias. And what is the right way to go.

May we take up the perpetual invitation to connect to the Divine through pausing to pray. May we seek right judgement as opposed to only seeking what is right for us, our group or ego. And may we sleep soundly and safely each night.
Amen

Second chances
(And third. And fourth. And fifth.)

I mess up all the time. Most of the time I know soon after I mess up, that I've messed up. There are times I even know I'm messing up as I'm messing up. And if I'm honest, I'd have to say that sometimes I know before I mess up that what I'm about to do/say will be messing up even before I do/say it.

I need a daily second chance. Jesus, when asked about forgiveness, said that we should forgive those who mess up not 7 times, not 70 times but..... loads more that 70 times. I think he meant we should forgive times infinity. And if we are called to that, God forgives continually. I heard once (in Lough Derg of all places) that we don't even need to ask for forgiveness for God to forgive- we need to ask for forgiveness so that we can experience that forgiveness in ourselves (deep eh?!).

So, I pray for second chances for me. And for you. I pray that if I need to give you a second chance that I'll be moved to do so. And I know that the God of all love, mercy and compassion is waiting for us all to experience God's great love- the ultimate second (third, fourth, fifth etc) chance.
Amen

Reflection on a mountain top walk

I spent some hours today walking to the summit of Divis Mountain here in Belfast. It was the most windy day I've walked in for a very long time. Depending on what direction I was going, the wind was variously at my back, in my face, pushing me from the side. It became the dominant feature of my walk today. As always when walking alone my thoughts turned to God and in particular today, to the spiritual life. I learned a great deal and I'd like to share a few thoughts if that's ok.

Walking into the wind:
When walking into the wind, the only thing kept me going was resolve. It would have been very tempting to stop walking altogether (but that would only have delayed the inevitable journey – there were no rescue helicopters!). I kept a sense of focus on my journey and, in particular, on my destination. Most of the time, I could not see my destination. What I could see, however, was the scenery on the way. Even facing into the wind and all the effort it took, could not take away from the beauty of the world and people around me. Realising this also helped strengthen my resolve to keep travelling on to my destination.

It would have been very tempting (and understandable) for me to want the wind to 'go away'. But walking into the wind takes more effort, burns more calories, builds more muscle and stamina. It's good to walk into the wind!

And besides, the wind that I experienced as blowing into my face and pushing me back, was the same wind that was another's back and was helping them along. The wind is not mine to control, nor to fully fathom. It is my task to accept that there is wind.

When the wind died down:
At the summit of the mountain, the wind was at its strongest. There were times that it nearly blew me off my feet. And yet, when I walked only a few feet down from the summit the wind died down completely. It wasn't that there was no wind anywhere. No. It was only that I had come to a spot on the journey where there was shelter from the wind. I felt a sense of calm come over me. My body, which had felt so cold in the wind, began to heat up a little. I could take a moment to look around and to give thanks for the journey I was on. I reflected that there were many other times I had walked on this mountain when there was no wind. I did not have the same sense of thankfulness however that I experienced today in that spot. Other times I took for granted the moments of calm – not even seeing them as such. It took the wind today to help me appreciate the calm times. Thank God!

With the wind at my back:
On the final climb up to the summit, there is a path made of rocks. It's an awkward path at times. Today it was icy in places, water-filled in others. The rocks can be bit treacherous. However, today at this point the wind was at my back. It literally pushed me up the path. I still had to do the climbing, but with the wind at my back the climb seemed more doable; less a chore more an opportunity to climb higher. I reflected on what keeps the wind at my back in life. Here are some of those things:
Prayer – both saying prayers and talking with God
Going to Mass
Reading
Consuming sensibly (food, drink, buying things, internet, media)
Relating well to others
Being curious
Acknowledging my need of God

When I do these things and others the wind is at my back. I still have to put an effort into life, but I can see life as opportunity rather than chore.

I'm back down the mountain now but I can feel the wind still in my bones. I feel the effort I put in, in the muscles in my legs and back. And I pray that these reflections will help me to move along the right path- in union with God, forever speaking of his wonder and forever in love with all people.
Amen

Fear, anxiety and desolation

Might sound like a strange prayer, but let me tell you about a recent experience of mine.

One night, after going to bed, I found that I could not sleep. I tossed and turned. I prayed for a while. I thought happy thoughts. All the things that I knew brought restful sleep. But to no avail.

As the night went on, I began to enter into a period of feeling really bad. It's hard to explain. I felt fear – fear about my life; fear about dying. I worried about things I hadn't worried about in a long time. I felt really lost. It was a dreadful (dread-filled) experience. And it went on for hours.

As the wee small hours of the night became the early hours of the morning, I must have drifted off into fitful sleep. When the alarm woke me up, though, I woke with a prayer on my lips. I remember saying over and over in my mind:
I can't do this alone, Lord. I need you. I can't do this alone, I need you.

The feelings of fear and anxiety were gone, but I was unsettled for the next day or so. Over the following days, I reflected on my experience that night. I really feel I was in a moment of desolation – feeling distant from God; distant from who I really am; filled with horrible emotions. However, the waking prayer has been something I learned a great deal from.

I realised once again that I am only complete and whole when I am in union with the Divine; when I recognise that I need God to be with me. And when I realise this and take some time in prayer to build that relationship, fear and anxiety leave me.

May we be comforted in our times of desolation. May we learn from those times. May we recognise that we need One greater than ourselves to make this journey all it can be.
Amen

The giving of a gift

Is there one gift you could commit to giving in this time to God?
How about:
One prayer of thanksgiving
One act of charity
One kind word spoken to someone in need
One book on spirituality read
One church service attended
One practical act of help to another
One person forgiven
One request for forgiveness
One prejudice confronted
I'm gonna give it a go.
Amen

Thanksgiving for pets

We got Jenny the wee black dog in June 2007. She was just nine months old and we got her from the pound. Getting her came a the end of a lengthy enough period of time trying to convince my wife Nuala that it would be a good idea (this is a theme in our marriage!). She agreed and we got Jenny.

The background to us getting Jenny is rather a sad one, though. The previous year my best friend Fearghal had died. This was a very traumatic loss for all of his family and friends; myself included. My life often felt a little empty in the months following his death. I was grieving and struggled for a while.

I am blessed with many good friends and a great family and I had company. But something was missing.

And so, when we got Jenny, I realised that spending time with her helped. She had spent her short life cooped up in a flat with her owner and two other dogs. He owner did her best and did love Jenny. However, ultimately she couldn't cope and she gave Jenny up. As a result of her life to date, when we got Jenny she couldn't walk on a lead; she wasn't socialised around other dogs; she had no sense of the rules of family life. I had to (and wanted to) spend a lot of time with her. And boy did it pay off! She has turned out to be the best dog in the world. And in the months that followed I became happier and began to heal- through prayer, the love of my family and friends and the company of Jenny.

I have a lovely memory of sitting at my back door on a late summer's evening, with a glass of red wine and Jenny at my feet. I felt at peace for the first time in a while. And now I have Madadh the great dane with me as well. Two good buddies. Two fiends who have walked literally hundreds of miles with me as I think, pray, watch, listen, talk with others, work things out. And I am grateful for their company. May we come to know the love of our pets. May we return that love, and care for them responsibly. And may God bless you all this night.
Amen

The wisdom of age

While walking one morning in the Falls Park, I met a woman I've know for some years now. I hadn't seen her in many months and it was great to bump into her. She's a woman well into her 70s. She told me about all she's up to at the minute. Safe to say, she's not letting age stand in the way of her experiencing life. She's just finished a counselling course; she's working at an after schools project; she's part of a telephone support line.

But what struck me about her was that she had many exciting (and radical) views on faith, God and church. She revelled in telling me the spiritual insights she had garnered since we last met. She longed for a more just, unified and peaceful world. She saw God in everything and God's plan at work everywhere- especially in chaos. She felt that God was moving us all to a better future. She did, however, realise that this would cause pain and suffering, worry and anxiety to many who did not want to be challenged by God; those who prefer the status quo to transformation.

I left the conversation almost breathless through excitement at her ideas. They have stayed with me all day. I was blessed by our meeting.

May we seek out the wisdom of the older generation. May we take care of those who are old and in need. And may we be open enough to consider that God's plan may involve radical change for our views on faith, our churches and our lives.
Amen

The patience of the grower

Every year for the past six or seven years we have had our family holiday in beautiful Lagos, Portugal. We have made many great friends there by now and the place is very special to us all.

I've got to know the countryside around Lagos quite well by walking and cycling through it on a daily basis while there. It's full of smells, sounds and sights that do this city dweller the world of good!

One of my regular routes takes me past a series of small holdings in various states of repair and productivity. I have been taken with one of these in particular over the years.

When I first walked past it, it was really run down. The small house was unoccupied. The brickwork was poor. The land was only a small, thin strip and nothing grew there. It was baked orange and barren.

A couple of years ago I noticed that there was some work going on. The fence around the property had been mended and the house looked more lived in.
Subsequently, over the years, each time I go back the little farm get more and more developed. This year, there was an irrigation system working away and there was a grid of different patches of land producing melon, figs and other fruit as well as some vegetables.

What bad been barren was now heavy with produce. What had looked tired and finished now looked vibrant and working. It is really beautiful. I look forward to seeing it this coming year, please God.

It strikes me that this transformation was not a quick one. It took years. It took money. It took hard labour. Most of all, it took the patience of someone who knew how these things develop. I am in awe of it.

May we look to see what could do with transforming in our own lives. May we seek always to use the gifts and talents we have in the most productive way possible (for the good of others). May we come to know the patience needed for real transformation. And may we work in sync with the Grower; the One who sows the seeds in our lives.
Amen

Coming through the fog

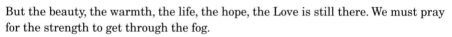

I took this picture up on Divis Mountain. Where there should have been a long clear shot of beautiful countryside, full of life, there was freezing fog. The air was cold and biting; the ground treacherously slippery.
It's not that the countryside had changed. It wasn't that the plants or animals weren't there. They were. If I'd taken the photo today at the same spot I'd have seen that.
Our lives can seem all fog and slippery slopes sometimes. We can feel that the very essence of life itself is far away or gone. We can feel cold, frozen even.

But the beauty, the warmth, the life, the hope, the Love is still there. We must pray for the strength to get through the fog.
Amen

New life

Christmas Eve when I was growing up was a day and night filled with a sense of expectation, excitement and ritual (the Christmas turkey being put into the oven to cook overnight, filling the house with a beautiful smell; early to bed in case Santa didn't come!). It was a special day that left me in no doubt that the next day was even more special.

And then Christmas Day itself was a day of new things. We had new clothes. We had new toys. We ate food we didn't get at other times of the year. We went to Mass and there were huge crowds all dressed in their finest. Hands were shaken with vigour. People hugged and smiled. It all felt bright and shiny and new.

And how fitting it was. Newness is what Christmas was and still is all about. Each year we celebrate God made human; born as a boy into this world. Awesome stuff. On Christmas Morning this year I invite you to reflect on your life as it is now. Not as how you want it to be. Just as it is. Be thankful for those people, situations and things you have in your life.

And then think of a few things in your life that could with being renewed.
For example:

A commitment to a relationship
Effort at work
Prayer life
Self-care
Giving to charity
A life giving hobby
As the God-child came to renew the face of the Earth, so this Christmas you can renew your life and commit to living well. A prayer along the way may even help you in that!!
Amen

Real love

A phrase has been ringing in my ears all day so I'll share it as my prayer tonight: Stop trying to change people and get busy loving them.

So often our position in relationships and in religious stance as well can be driven by a desire to change people. I wonder what motivates this? Sometimes I'm sure we have the best outcome for the other person/group in mind. But other times I fear it's not so righteous.

Sometimes it's driven by dogma, theory, insecurity, power, our own need to be validated. And it can lead to needless conflict, relationship breakdown, exclusion, gang-making, self worship, hurt.

I'm not saying that no one needs to change ever. Change is inevitable and, at times necessary. But true change (the type of change that an encounter with God brings about) can only be a product of being loved first. Until I am loved, I won't know what love is. Until I know what love is, I won't see a purpose in life. Until I see a purpose in life, I won't look to how I live. Until I look to how I live and then love others more, I won't change.

May we love first. And love last. And love all the way in between. Surely that's what the incarnation of God among us is all about?
Amen

Letting go

I had a very poignant conversation one day with a friend who was coming into his first Christmas after his mother's death. He recounted the story of the moment of her death.

He told me that when she died, the many wrinkles, worry lines and general stressed look on her face slowly smoothed out. What had looked like permanent features of her face actually were not. They were symptoms of ill health, of smoking cigarettes, of stress and worry. And when they went, she looked beautiful. She looked peaceful. She looked happy.

It really struck me that there are so many things I hold on to as if they are just permanent features of life or inevitable things in life- features and things that cause me concern, worry and stress – that are no such thing. I'm sure they leave their mark on me. Either on my face, or on my psyche, or on my soul.

I wonder if it will take me until the moment of my death to realise what they are and to finally let go of them? Or will I grow in wisdom, grace and strength and see them for what they are and let them go?

May we see things in our lives for what they really are. May we see the things that are damaging and let them go. And may we take time to slow down, reflect and refocus our lives.
Amen

Those things that cannot be spoken

Most of us will have things close to our hearts that we would find it hard to speak out loud. These will be intensely personal things. Things that give rise to strong emotions. Things that are of our very essence.

Speaking them out loud might leave us feeling very vulnerable or even ashamed. However, we can acknowledge these things. We can resolve what needs to be resolved. Usually, though, this can only happens when we share them. And once shared, they cease to have the power they had over us.

So tonight I'm praying for the strength to share what I need to share and to resolve what I need to resolve. I'm praying for the things you could share and resolve. I'm praying for you and the gift you are (I hope you know that coz it's true). And I'm praying that this time can be a time of real growth as we wait patiently for the Coming.
Amen

Learning

The world that seemed so certain to me as a young man....seems a little less certain now. As a lot of us men experienced, I thought I knew a lot as a younger man. At times it may have led to a bit of arrogance and definitely to me taking life a lot less seriously (and preciously) than I might have.

As I get older, I see how much I don't know. This can lead to a few reactions:

I can rebel and revert to less grown up modes of thinking. I can simply fool myself that I know more than I do. I can tell myself that I have this life thing all worked out. I can tell myself that I need nothing; only me and what I know and experience. I can put the blinkers on. I can tell myself that if I don't understand something it is either not important or even that it doesn't exist at all.

I can get depressed and anxious. I can tell myself that life is un-knowable and there-fore dangerous and to be avoided, save for my narrow field of vision and a small range of 'safe' experiences. In this mode, not only do I not need anything outside of me and what I know; anything outside of this is dangerous and not to be trusted.

Or...
I can acknowledge that there are many things that I don't know. There are many things about life that I do not understand. I can accept this and think it is OK. I can be humble and think, 'why should I need to understand everything? Does life need me to understand everything for life to be complete?'

From this stand point I can then set my self (ego) aside and search for the realities of life from a position of freedom. From here I can free myself up to learn.
Like you, I have learned a few things through my life (I've discounted most of what I learned in arrogant, rebellious, blinkered and depressed mode). I can only relate to others the things I have learned for myself. And offer them as invitations to some-thing bigger; something good; something awesome in fact. I hold onto these as some of my central realities:

there is a God – seriously there is
God loves me – Yes, God love God for God's generosity but I believe God does
God loves you – seriously. Let that be true to you for one minute and tell me you're not changed
life is tough – but most good things are some times
there is more to life than simply living for me

May we come to know that we all have lots to learn. May we see this as an opportunity, not as a threat. May we look at life as something to be embraced in all of its difficulties as well as all its joys. And may you know tonight that God loves you- totally, unconditionally.
Amen

The good we see all around us

It's easy to get caught up in thinking that the world is only the hurt we see, the problems we experience or the bad news we read. I'm not saying that there is no hurt or badness in the world. Of course there is. But that's not the whole story. It's so much more than that.

Everywhere I look I see good people. People who do good things. People who 'be' good people. I am amazed and humbled by it every day. Let me give you some examples.

All around me on facebook there are:
people who are doing fundraising
people who post heartfelt pleas for justice and peace
people who are asking for prayers for themselves and others
videos to make us smile, laugh or think
people trying to work the world out

In my real world life I see these things too. I also see:
acts of selflessness and charity
people struggling with illness who smile anyway
people dying with dignity
people carrying all sorts of worries with great strength
people praying constantly
people challenging us to be better
people holding up a mirror to hypocrisy and injustice
people calling for righteous change

Even when my life is a real struggle and I get down I must remember:
music is life giving
the sun shines every day
the rain washes the streets clean
trees, grass and flowers look amazing
animals are beautiful
I have a family and friends who love me

God loves me (if that doesn't speak of how gracious and forgiving God is, then nothing will) and God loves you and the people we don't/can't love
– EVERYBODY WITHOUT EXCEPTION
The whole story is not complete without recognition of the good. Recognition of possibility. Recognition of God's love.

May you see the good news all around you. May you have support, comfort and Consolation in the bad times. May we reach out and be love to those less fortunate than
us. And may God bless us all this night.
Amen

Those nearing death

Some of us here will know of people coming to the end of their life. This can be a
time of great worry, distress and fear for the people themselves and for those around
them.

May those nearing the end of their journey here in this world feel a sense of Com-
fort, calm and peace. May those close to them be consoled in their worry. And may
God bless us all tonight.
Amen

P.S. Hug those close to you more often. Tell them you love them. Laugh at their
jokes. Be interested in their stories. Listen to their worries. Hold them close.
Tonight. Tomorrow. Every day.

Being heard

I had the experience recently of being really listened to. Someone sat quietly and listened to the answer I gave to a question she asked me. It was a deep question and it
required a complex answer. Not only that, but it was so complex that in my answer I
rambled my way along a few different paths until I got to the point (a point that I
didn't know I was going to make until I had made it actually).

It was only while reflecting on this experience that I realised that in this conversation, there were very few times when the person I was with spoke. Mostly, she was
quiet and listened. I came away from the conversation feeling... listened to, I guess.
But more than that; I felt I learned something about myself and about the things I
was asked about. It was a good experience. And although she didn't speak, the person I was with was co-responsible with me for this.

What a gift we give when we listen. Not listen for a gap in the conversation to jump into to. Not listen for things we like/dislike. Not listen for approval/disapproval. Just listen. What we say when we say little rings loud.

May you have people in your life who really listen to you. May you realise that you have things that are worth being listened to and the bravery to say them. May we find the balance between talking and listening to those we come into contact with. And may we come to realise that in God we have One who always listens and always wants to hear from us.
Amen

The flow

There are two competing realities in my life – the nature of things and my experience of things. I'll start with the second first (wouldn't be me!).

I often experience things through a particular lens. That lens is all to do with my story (history) of life, my story of me and my story of others. And the lens can vary depending on where I am in relation to those stories. Let me give you an example. When I am tired and/or stressed I experience things very often as irritants or as pressure. When my lens is not tiredness or stress, I experience the same things differently. Take a request to do an errand for someone. Tired lens: 'not again', 'why me', 'typical', 'no'. Not so tired lens: 'yes'.

When I am down I experience things as simply confirming my own sadness or lack of self esteem. A comment made to or about me suddenly takes on added (even profound) meaning when I have the lens of depression, anxiety or feeling low. And yet it is the same comment that I shrug off or even grow from when viewed through a different lens; one of feeling more secure in my self and my esteem.

My experience of things can become to me the Gospel truth of the nature of those things. I can lose sight of the fact that there are many factors that influence my experience of things and that it is the experience of things that often cause me trouble rather than the things themselves.

While my experience of things varies and is influenced by me and others in my life, the nature of things is constant. It simply is. The request to do an errand is simply a request. A comment to or about me is simply words. If I stick with the nature of things, I am in a better position to decide how I might respond to them. I'm less caught up in my initial temptation to see them through my own lens. Through a certain lens life can seem:
Tough
Sad
Pointless
Cruel
Better without me

While it is true that we can experience life like this at times, the nature of life is a bigger story. It is more than our current experience of it. Even if I am caught in experiencing life in one or more of the ways above, the nature of life is such that these things will end and life will once again be full of endless possibility. We limit the nature of our life by viewing it through our lens and telling ourselves (or believing when we are told) that 'this is all there is'. And yet, God wants us to have life and have it 'to the full', not simply our version of what that full life can be. And suddenly, when we realise all of this we see life is:
Possibility
Love filled
Endless
To be lived to the full
Better when shared with others
Sacred

Look at the river in the picture. Is it calm and glassy? Or is it wild and running fast? Depending on how I look at the picture I can say either and experience it as correct. The truth is... It is a river, flowing according to its nature. And your nature is one of complete goodness. Go with the flow.
Amen

Really living

There are seasons in all of our lives. If we pay attention to life, sometimes we can see the patterns and identify the season we're in. When we do that it can heighten our awareness of the meaning in life events and in the possibilities for learning that God might be inviting us to.

I've had a phrase in my mind all day today. It kinda jumped into consciousness this morning (in the shower of all places) and has fascinated me ever since. I'll share it with you:
Standing close to death and yet, to live.

It helped me see something about the season of life I am in. It's one of dying. Not personally, yet. I've had the experience of knowing people who have died or have found out about their impending death recently. More than usual it seems. It's been sad – I learned about the death by suicide of a man I've known for years only today – and worrying. But I wonder if, not running away from the sadness and worry (which are real), could I be in the presence of opportunities learn and grow (up)?

In the company of death I am drawn to ask myself, 'am I really living?' And what might 'really living' be?

The temptation and easy way out is to think about all the creative and self serving ways I could use my money and time- holidays, computers, gadgets, clothes, cars, food, property. That would be 'really living' wouldn't it? Would it? That would be living really comfortably alright. But 'really living'? I don't know. A younger me in a different season might have said,' yes'.

What are the marks of 'really living'? Draw your own conclusions. But I have had some thoughts that I'll share. Really living might include:
Taking care of my body
Taking care of my mind
Reading beautiful books
Loving myself more
Looking for those who have less and giving them some of my 'stuff'
Crying with the hurt
Talking to God every day
Spending less time on line and more in the 'real world'
Forgiving people

Quietening my own desires in favour of hearing others'
Visiting lonely people
Laughing till I cry
Crying till I can laugh again

May we take time to see and be in the seasons of our lives. May we comfort the bereaved and help the ill. And may we be alive to the possibility of really living.
Amen

The last cut...or not

I was walking (again) in the Falls Park and got into a conversation with a man there about the unseasonably mild weather we have been experiencing this year. He said that the grass in the park has had its 'last cut' three times. He explained that the park attendants give the grass a last cut before the winter sets in. Each of the three times this year they have done this, the weather has brightened and the temperature has gone up and the grass has begun to grow again.

I got this vision of the grass thinking it was all over and then suddenly this heat, this energy flows through it and off it goes again. Growing up higher and greener than ever.

Have you ever felt like you've had your 'last cut'? Like life has thrown too much at you? Like things are never going to be good again? We typically feel this in times of relationship breakdown, job loss, illness, death or addiction. What else has given you your 'last cut' feeling?

My conversation today has reminded me that there is always the possibility that what feels like a dead end, no hope situation can be turned round (we've all probably had some small or not so small examples of this in our own lives).

It reminded me that in those moments of crying out to God, 'why?' or 'help!' and letting go, we often experience the surge of energy the grass got. The surge of hope; the energy of the helping hand of others; the grace to get through. To grow again.

May you experience the warmth of love and the energy of renewal when you experience a 'last cut' moment. May we seek to be the love that others need in their moments of pain and trial. And may God bless you with every grace and all strength that you need this night.
Amen

Perspective

These two photos are of the same scene. Both taken in the same place and only a few seconds separate them.

In one, the foreground is bright and clear. In the other the foreground is dark and unclear. Foreboding even. But the light in the sky is sharper and somehow stronger. All I did was change the angle of the shot by millimeters. Both are the same physically. Just a little change of perspective changes how we see things.

May we look twice at our lives. On first look it might seem dark. However, on our second look we might see the strong Light we have to lead us. And maybe we can change our perspective to see that things can be brighter than they first seem. *Amen*

I was reflecting on the Our Father today

Our Father: God is as intimate in relationship to us as a good father. The word Jesus used was 'Abba'. This is more like 'daddy'. Praying for all fathers. Old and young. May we love our children with a perfect love.

In heaven: This world is not all there is. This world is not perfect because it cannot be so. Our ideas of afterlife and of heaven are probably very varied. But one thing is for sure- our closest approximation is so far away from the reality. But a reality it is. Chew on that one for a while. It will give hope.

Hallowed by your name: What do I hold hallowed, holy, privileged, special in my life? Is it God? Is it others' needs? Or is it myself? Do I set myself up as my own God and worship at the temple of pleasure and short-term gratification?

Your kingdom come: God's kingdom is at once here and now and at the same time it is yet to come. We will only witness fully the kingdom when all are united with God. It's a mystery that we can only dwell in and contemplate. And from that contemplation, we must act to bring about the kingdom of God. Some signs of that? Peace, unity, love, justice.

Your will be done on earth as it is in heaven: Do I accept that I have no control over life and let go? Do I accept that God is in the driving seat? Or do I still hold on to the false self that says, 'I must be in control'. For 'thy will' to be done, 'my will' must be gone as Fr Richard Rohr says.

Give us each day our daily bread: This is at once a recognition that my daily bread (that which I need to live my life) is given from God and also that I should ask each day only for those things I need to get by. Not 'give us this day our daily laptops, tablets, second cars, Xboxes'. All of these things are not bad. But they are bonuses that not all have and that we should be thankful for.

And forgive us our wrongdoing: I move along a bad path at some time of every day. I have wronged people and myself. I humbly ask for forgiveness of anyone I have hurt. And I seek to do good.

As we forgive those who have wronged us: With each breath in I breathe in God's love and as I breathe out I breathe out forgiveness for any wrong that has been done to me. I forgive all who have wronged me and I don't need anyone to ask for forgiveness to do so.

And lead us not into temptation: I prefer the translation that says, 'and let us not be led into temptation'. I don't have the image of a God just waiting to throw us a curve ball or trip us up. Our temptation usually comes from ourselves or others we know. Or from the dominant narrative in society: 'you can have what you want, when you want it. And if someone tells you otherwise- get rid of them'.

But deliver us from evil: God, be with me when I am tempted. Be with me when I am wronged. Be with me when I am ill. Be with me when I am called on to be brave. Be with me when it is difficult to love. Deliver me from my weakness. Deliver me from the hurtful and damaging actions of others. Deliver me from apathy. Deliver me from the status quo.

Amen

The light to come

I took this picture at the top of the hill in the Falls Park, Belfast. It's one of my favourite places in the world. The rain was off (how Northern Ireland is it to notice when it's NOT raining?!) and the wind was soft and the park was quiet. I had time to be with myself and God.

I saw this sight and snapped it. It said a lot to me.

In the dark skyline I could see houses and electricity pylons that reminded me of every day life. The 'ordinary' stuff. The grind as they say. The day to day rhythm of my life. I recalled the people I am blessed to know. Those who bring me consolation. Those who challenge me. Those I love and who love me. I thought of you here, who I connect with on this page and yours.

I could also see trees and I was reminded of the wonders of this world. Walking every day I get to see the most marvellous sights: trees, flowers, squirrels, rats, birds, my beloved dogs. What a beautiful world it is. If we could only appreciate and love it.

I could see the dark areas. Areas I knew were full of something. But something I couldn't see and didn't know in that moment. That reminded me of how small I am. That what I do know is so much smaller than what I don't know.

I could see a Church spire. This reminded me of the life I now lead. A life of journeying with and in faith. Of being ever more drawn to serve and love those about me. And above it all? I could see the light. Bursting powerfully over the whole picture. There is better to come. There is light after darkness. There is meaning. There is an end it hurt. There is unity. There is Love.

All we have to do is really open our eyes and see it.
Amen

The absence of loved ones

This is a photo of my left foot. I got the purple and red sun-like tattoo in late May 2006. Earlier that month my friend, Fearghal McConnell, died suddenly. It was a very sad moment in my life (and the lives of many other too). I got the tattoo as a memorial of him.

The design is one that I have in three places on my body. Each is slightly different because the rays of the sun in each represent different people. The first of these is on my left arm and has a 'ray' for my immediate family – brothers, sisters, my wife Nuala and the kids, my parents and grandparents.

The second is on my right leg, slightly above the outside ankle bone. It has extra rays for people who had passed away and who I missed.

The third, then, is the one in the picture and one of the rays is for Fearghal (I've stopped getting that design tattooed because I've got old enough to have lost so many close people in death that the tattoo would be too big).

If you look closely, you can see that at the base of one of the rays, there is a circular gap in the ink. That came about because some years ago, I surfed fairly regularly. I was also beginning to develop tendinitis in my left knee which meant that as I popped up on the board from lying down to standing, I dragged my left leg a bit. That, in turn, meant that I dragged my left foot across the board, causing my foot to bleed. Many times I came out of the water with a bloody foot. Over time, It became scarred and removed some of the ink from the tattoo.

It strikes me as kinda appropriate, though. There is an absence of ink in the tattoo. It is incomplete. It's missing something. Just in the same way, that I feel the absence of Fearghal (and many others now). I miss him, and them, like a tattoo misses a little bit of its ink. A little bit of the picture is gone.

The second picture is of a guitar. My friend, Kevin McGreevy was approached by a colleague this week and she asked him to do up this guitar which was in need of a bit of tender loving care. It had, she explained, lay in her attic for the last 8 years. She had inherited it from a cousin who had died and forgot about it until discovering it again last week. She knew Kevin would be the man to do it up.

She went on to tell Kevin about how the cousin who had died had several guitars but that most had gone now and she didn't know where. Except for one. A steel guitar from the 1930s. She told Kevin, 'his friend got that as a memory of my cousin'. Kevin tells me the hair stood up on his neck. 'What did you call your cousin'. 'You wouldn't have known him', came the reply. 'Was it Fearghal by any chance'. The woman was astounded that Kevin knew this. He explained that he knew me and that I had inherited a steel guitar eight years ago from my friend who died. My friend was her cousin. Remarkable.

Kevin did me the honour of passing the guitar to me to fix. And so it came to pass that eight years after his death I was holding and fixing and polishing my old friend's guitar. I also plugged it in and played some of the songs he and I played together back in the 'old days'. It sounded like him. As I held the guitar, I knew I was holding him and that he was holding me too.

May we never forget those who have passed away from this life. May we keep our eyes open for the things still here that can remind us of them. May we love those we still have in our lives. And may we come to know that for those who have died, this life has changed, not ended and that we will meet again.
Amen

Thank you Kevin. You made an old man remember good times.

The right type of busy-ness

I'm busy. A lot of the time, I'm too busy. But in a way, I'm not busy enough. Let me explain.

I love working. I love doing things. A lot of the time, the things I do are good for me and good for others. I've worked hard at that last bit through the years (my focus when I was younger was more often on what I thought was good for me than on what was good for others). Other times, the things I do are not so good for me at all. Overall, my life involves a lot of doing.

And when a life involves a love of doing things, that life gets busy. Busy doing things. That life can become all about doing things. And then, when there are no things to do, that life can feel stressful and then we look for things to do to relieve the stress of having nothing to do. Familiar? I'd say it is familiar for some, but unfamiliar for others.

The irony is that a life focussed on doing things will deliver stress two ways. Firstly, the stress of not having something (else) to do. We get agitated. We feel useless. We expend energy in finding things to do. What things? It doesn't matter. Just things! Secondly, there is the stress of having used all of our energy doing things! Busyness breeds tiredness. And tiredness uninterrupted breeds stress and, eventually, burn out.

So, my prayer tonight is for a different type of busyness. (I've got the 'doing' busyness all sown up). I want to get busy 'being'. So, here are a few 'being' commitments:
Taking a break
Sleeping enough
Eating well
Praying
Not talking
Seeing the world around me
Praying
Spending time laughing with my family and friends
Playing snooker
Praying
Playing guitar
Feeling the wind on my face
Talking to my wife
Praying
Listening to 70s and 80s music (The Cure are my current favourite)
Writing without editing
Thinking
Praying

Did I mention praying?
I am a human being. I am also a human doing. I like doing. But I 'do' better when I take care of 'being'. I'm going to get busy 'being'. Who's up for it?
May we all take time alone, in silence regularly. In that silence I am with God. I respect whatever your beliefs are around the existence of God, but so does God. May we all do what we can, when we can, to help others and be genuinely good to ourselves. And may we develop a good balance of 'being' and 'doing'.
Amen

The crushed

I was with a colleague and we walked past a Rosemary plant. I told her to pick a leaf and smell it. She did, but she couldn't smell anything. I realised that she was smelling the whole leaf and that in order to smell the aroma she needed to crush the leaf. The act of crushing the leaf releases the oils. And these, in turn, release the aroma of Rosemary. And the smell is powerful.

There are so many times in our lives when people feel crushed. Times of worry, stress, illness, grief, loss, relationship difficulties. Yet it's at those very times in our lives that we can see humans at their best.

Have a think about the people you know who faced their impending death with a fearlessness and dignity that astounded and inspired you.

Remember someone who reached out to you when you were in need and really made a difference to you.

Think about someone who lives with pain in body or mind and who does so without complaining at all and continues to love and support others.

Call to mind the times when you saw someone crushed in their life and did something awesome to alleviate their difficulties.

Think about the times in your life when you have been crushed in some other way. Really call these times to mind and see that, in the midst of the pain and worry, something powerful or soothing or inspiring also happened. This is difficult to do. Especially if the experience that crushed you was very traumatic.

But it seems that the most powerful acts of human (even superhuman) caring and loving come at the most powerfully crushing moments this life throws at us. Sometimes, in our own difficult crushing moments we can surprise ourselves by being better people than we usually are. Strange, I know. But true, I think.

May we reach out to those who are crushed and offer them Soothing, Love and Care. May we, in our moments of being crushed, realise that there are at the same time some powerful moments of beauty, support, energy and grace being released. And may we continue to grow in our love for one another. God bless.
Amen

The wisdom of the young

I was playing a gig last night with my son Brendan. It was a real blast. We played really well. At the end of the gig I said to him, 'we should have got someone to video that so we could watch it back'.

In reply he said, 'ah well, we'll just have to live for the moment'.

Wow! He was telling me so much right there. He was saying that we should just play the music for the moment the sound came out. For the experience of hearing it as we played it. For the people we were playing for. For the joy of playing together.
But he told me much more. He told me that;
This moment right now is eternal.
This moment is unique and never to be repeated.
This moment doesn't know or care what has happened before or what is going to happen in the future.
This moment is ripe with possibility.
This moment is where we experience love.
This moment is where we build what is to come.
This moment is where it's at!

May we listen to the wisdom of the young. May we live each moment to the full. And may we not get caught up in judging the past and predicting the future.
Amen

For the end

Walking round the streets today, I saw so many houses decked out in bright lights with trees and decorations visible inside. It definitely felt like the start of a new time of year. And so it is, of course.

So today I've been reflecting on newness again. It's a bit of a theme for me at the minute, I know. Today is the first day in a new Church year for us Catholics. Today is the start of Advent. Tomorrow is the first day of a new month. The leaves on the trees are splendid in their new brown colour. So much newness around us today. And yet, for something new to happen, something must end. And so the month of November ends tonight. The old Church year ended yesterday. The green leaves had to change colour or fall off.

In my life, I'm much better at celebrating the newness and being appreciative of it, than recognising the ending of old things as necessary precursors to the newness- no ending of the old, no beginning of the new. I more often than not lament the endings. I feel disappointed, sad, wistful, depressed even. How about you?

My children growing up is a good example. I can get sad and wistful about them not being small any more. I can miss their little baby voices and sayings. I can worry about them becoming much more independent. Or I can see all of that as the necessary ending of one stage of their lives as they grow into other new ones. Once I do that I am much freer to marvel at the people they are becoming. Free from (ego driven) regrets and melancholy.

For people of faith, we are challenged to think the same about the ultimate ending-death. We are invited to see death as a necessary precursor to something else – something much more. We are called to believe it so deeply as to be able to say – life has changed, not ended. Tough when faced with a bereavement. But no less true for that.

Another thought struck me: I wonder what I could seek to end in my life now, that would facilitate a beautiful and exciting new beginning? Am I too wrapped up in looking for ways of comfort and self satisfaction to see the areas of life that could (should?) end?

May we see endings in their proper context. May we grieve those we have lost in the knowledge that true Life never ends. May we look with honesty at our lives and seek the endings that will bring new life to us.
Amen

Newness

I've been reflecting on 'newness'. I've been drawn to think about little newborn children. Take a moment and conjure the image of a newborn child in your mind. See the little one. The face, arms, hands. Feel the softness of the skin and smell that 'newborn smell'.

For many, the immediate reaction when faced with such a little creation is to want to hold him/her, to cuddle, to feel connected. It's remarkably strong in many of us. I wonder why?

Psychologists would tell us, I think, that it is a biological reaction resulting in a good attachment for the infant and a caregiver, designed to assure the continuation of the species. Yep, I hear that. But it's more, isn't it?

I think it's because we see in the infant the purest expression of us: of humanity. The newborn is innocent; untouched and untarnished by experience of hurt, disappointment, judgement, selfishness, dissatisfaction, materialism, comparison with others. The new born is free.

And yet, each one of us ARE that newborn. We all came into the world in roughly the same manner, but exactly the same state: truly free. Wonderfully dependant on others and fearless in trusting.

Our experiences since....Well that's a different matter. We have all been tarnished by our own and others' transgressions. Tarnished and left feeling 'not new' by many difficult life experiences.

I am holding onto the fact that the newborn I once was is still the person I am and can be today. The newness of each day, the possibilities of life and the goodness of God are a reality. All I need to do is (as Jesus often said) 'be not afraid'. The opposite of fearing is not being courageous, brave, tough etc... It's having the ability to put our trust in others and in God.

Maybe if you look closely in the mirror and then search out a baby photo you will see the same features. And maybe, the same light in your eyes. What would that baby want you to do today? Tomorrow? The next day?

May all babies get the start in life they need. May we all connect each day to the pureness of humanity that we really are. And may the newness of Advent spread among us as we wait in expectation of Better things to come.
Amen

Part two
Poems for
the journey

For Our Sisters

(written the night the two Mercy Sisters, Frances and Marie died)

I stood tonight at the back door
I looked up at the clear night sky
And saw the stars
As I watched
New stars appeared
Each, I felt, for those
Who passed away today
They shone so brightly
I could smile

Belief

I believe in God.
I believe in a greater story than my own.
I believe that I have a (small) part in that bigger story.
I believe that I don't need to know the ins and outs of the bigger story.
I believe that I can understand my (small) part better
through prayer and meditation.
I believe that understanding others' needs
is more important than fulfilling my own desires.
I believe that no matter what, this life is precious from conception to death.
I believe that life can be filled with a mix of happiness and pain.
I believe that pain (while, at times horrible) is temporary.
I believe I need others to grow and grow up.
I believe everyone is invited to the party.
I believe that I will make mistakes.
I believe in Forgiveness.
I believe in Love.
I believe in God.

Good Friday
It's a sunny day today
Who would have thought that
On a day such as this
Blood could flow
The veil could be torn in two
The earth could shake
The tomb could await its faultless guest
It's peaceful here in the Falls Park
Birds call and old folk walk
Shakily but happily
Who would have thought that
On a day such as this
Suffering continues
Blood flows
Women and men die both
Peacefully and in torment
This path has been walked before
Good Friday

Easter Saturday
Each day begins
It happens
It ends
Predictable... not always
A new dawn brings no consolation
A sadness in the bones
He lies dead.... not always
The birdsong is noise
The sun's brightness somehow colder
Hopes and promises lie mortified... not always
Today is an empty day
Even the Church missing Presence
Emptiness endured... but not always
Holy Saturday

Rise – Easter Sunday

What will I allow to rise in me today?
Old hatred?
Old spite?
Old "poor me"?
Old hurts?
Old" I'm not worthy"?
Old falling out?
Or...
New joy?
New "can do"?
New reaching out?
New love?
New friendships?
New efforts?
New possibilities?
New laughter?
New helping?
New tolerance?
New acceptance?
New beginning?
New life?
Easter Sunday

I Will Always Smile At Your Name

I close my eyes, I see your face
May this vision never stop
You're teaching me the old songs like the old clothes shop
I see the pictures above the fire place
Pictures of our clan
And realise how much I owe you
You've made me what I am

Your laughter and your songs
In my memory live on
You're the reason that I'm here
And your life blood
It still flows in my veins
And I will always smile at your name

I remember our first walk together
I was eight years old
We walked the length of the Shaw's Road
In the bitter cold
It was tough and I was young
But still I struggled through
You see I wanted to be a big man
Just like you

Your laughter and your songs
In my memory live on
You're the reason that I'm here
And your life blood
It still flows in my veins
And I will always smile at your name

No more Sunday dinner sing songs
We'll have an empty seat
But I know you'll really be there
When we sit to eat
Your craic, your songs, your smile, your laughter
We will never hear
The life and soul of every party
The highlight of my year

Your laughter and your songs
In my memory live on
You're the reason that I'm here
And your life blood
It still flows in my veins
And I will always smile at your name

I close my eyes I see your face
Same vision till this day
Though you're gone your Spirit's wisdom
Still shows me the way
The years have passed I've grown older
But your face remains so clear
It still smiles to tell me 'my boy,
Don't worry I'm still near

Your laughter and your songs
In my memory live on
You're the reason that I'm here
And your life blood
It still flows in my veins
And I will always smile at your name

Unity

I close my eyes
I see clearly
That I am in you and
You in me
Though it seems impossible
We're told it is so
And now with eyes closed
And seeing clearly
I feel your presence and
Our unity

Being

Hope for what is to come.
Be in what is today.
Call on God to be with you.
Be patient and accept what comes.
Encourage others to do the same.
Begin by being.
Being with your self.
Being with others.
Being the self you are.
Being.
Begin.
Amen

The Fall

The rain falls
And so do I, daily
And yet it is
In falling that I see all
On my way down
All the lessons in mistakes
Learned from
All the wisdom in foolishness
Regretted
All the healing in wounds
Recovered from
All the possibility in hopelessness
Seen as finite
Falling down necessarily
To get back up

3-2-1

Seize the moment
You live
In

Acknowledge the power
You draw
From

Love the people
You exist
With

See the beauty
You walk
Through

Embrace the possibility
You run
To

Thank the Heavens
You dwell
Under

Sunday morning sadness

We party at the foot of the cross
No regard for those it calls to mind
Cider offered now where once
Was offered vinegar on a stick
We claim a mountain as 'ours'
Definitely not 'theirs'
Our messages only
As if the mountain cares
Graveyard scenes
Remembering the dead but
Teaching us more
About how we live today

Sometimes the rain stops

Sometimes the rain stops
And the clouds clear
But it takes me
Ten minutes to realise
That I'm walking in the sunshine
Ten minutes of needlessly walking
In the rain that's gone already
As if I'm Thomas doubting the sun (Son)
My body not registering
The warm glow
Of hope.

The Light Behind The Cloud

In every house, life
Goes on and by
Bills and spills and chills
And ill feeelings bring the cloud
The cloud, loud and imposing
Consumes our entire vision
Until it seems, not is
The only thing there
Cloudy days, cloudy nights
Fights, rights not respected
Threat of rain keeping us

Locked in sightless seeing
Thick cloud, real troubles
Rain does come, but some
The sky holds more
Than clouds I see
I see. I see only
When I open my eyes, my mind
To the whole story
This too will end, pain that is
And in real vision I'm free
To see, to be in delight
At the wholeness of being
In the light behind the cloud

Quietly Being

Moments of quiet
Seldom sought and yet
Yearning to be found
Leaving us clues to a better way
Of being

Moments of quiet
Loud with silence
Filled with insights that
Lead us to a purpose revealed
In being

Moments of quiet
Seeing differently
The ebb and flow of
Everyday events that hold us back
From being

Moments of quiet
Precious gifts hidden
In plain sight always
Available to be part of
Really being

A father's eyes

In a father's eyes shine bright
The memories of the childs growth
From birth to babe, to beginning
To spread their wings
Behind a father's eyes loom large
The moments of joy and sorrow
The moments of pride and regret
As life's journey winds on
Through a father's eyes it's clear
What a gift to the world all children are
The unbounded possibilities of their lives
Waiting to be fulfilled – watch out world!
In front of a father's eyes
The babies are no more
Dependence becomes inter-dependence
The caring goes both ways
For a father's eyes begin
To grow old and weak
And yet when they are closed in memory
The laughter of the children brings tears of joy

Giving

Give it up
Give it over
Give it all
Give it a go
Give it a rest
Give it one more try
Give it a chance
Give it time

The work at hand

How can we show them they're special?
How can we convince them we love them?
Those who feel that they are nothing
Who feel the weight of the world above them
The journey we take can be twisting
People can get caught up at every turn
The words and actions of others
Can cut, they can sting, they can burn
We're the nurses on a ward in a field hospital
On the battlefield that life can be
Watching out for the casualties around us
Who fall wounded – that's you and me
You see we're all in this together
There's simply no 'them and us'
Today it's someone's turn to be needy
And tomorrow it's mine to find someone I trust
The work at hand is lying before us
The opportunity to love never ends
To draw all into oneness and protection
Then wake up and begin to do it again
So how can we show them they're special?
We can start by seeing 'they're me'
Reaching out to hold all in tenderness
And being the Love we can be

Lent

Lent
Repent
Relent
Sins spent
Content?
No, sent
Lent

Arise
Rising
From sleep
From the darkness
Stretching
My body and mind
My soul; wide-eyed
Clothing myself
In the Love
That has won me
Truly awake
To the story
That is not me
Opening up
A new chapter
To play my part

Appreciation, raining down
Cold rain falling on a flat roof
Can you hear it?
The noise reminds me
That I am dry
Silent radiators burning
Oil and heating water
Do I realise
I am not cold?
Full fridge, Saturday's shopping
Sitting waiting
How lucky am I?
No hunger pangs
Cold rain falling on a flat roof
The machine gun noise
Shocks me into knowing
How blessed I am

Another day

Wake awake
See clearly
The gifts we have been given
To use each day
Yesterday with all its
Woes, trials or joys
Ended with nightfall
A memory, a lesson learned
Tomorrow unknown
We see as through
A glass, darkly
It's reality hidden, wisely
So today is all
Today is all
May we fall
Gently today into the hands of the living God

Surfing

Know that you are small
If in doubt swim in the sea and look up
A dot under the heavens
Swayed by an unseen current
Taken this way, then that
'There is no rhyme nor reason to this'
Being in it we feel at the mercy of unfathomable forces
With no sense to their movements
And yet, the tide come and goes
With regularity and purpose
And so it is with God
Deep, unfathomable, strong, big
We feel pulled this way and that
Constantly seeking to 'know'
But missing the flow of the current beneath, above, around us
I surfed a perfect wave once- perfect to me
I didn't fight the current or the swell
I didn't seek to know the facts
I sensed, I believed, I trusted
I stood on the board, went and felt alive

I met with Christ today

I met with Christ today
In the grieving family of a loved one lost
In the wind and rain and sunshine and grass
In the warm hug of a wife
In the words of encouragement of a friend
In the homeless man, dirty and tired
In the gay woman nursing her mother to death
In the opponent who attacked me
In the priest ordained 50 years alive with his 'new' church
In the song so beautiful I cried
In the wilderness of my inner doubting
In the midst of the terrible wars
In the pain and discomfort
In the bread, broken
I met with Christ today
Didn't you?

Grief

Grief
Felt in the gut
Bringing us back
To a child's state of being
Lost and alone
Grief
Felt through love
Ripped from the other
Rarely ready to let go
Just yet
Grief
Perfect space
To join another
To offer the ear, shoulder or arms
To walk in partnership
Grief
As with all things
This too will become part of the story
And we will grow and learn
The gift from the dying

The Story

Status: denied
Decried
Abhorred
Annihilated
Empowered
Risen
Eternal
Unified
Challenging
Welcoming
Status: loved

Beginning to breathe

Beginning to breathe
Involves a certain conscious effort
To teach the muscles how to heave
To teach the lungs how to convert
Once we learn we forget
The effort once expended
And the benefit of making that effort
In favour of unconscious breathing
And bad habits evolve
We breathe shallow, quick breaths
Missing the whole picture
The fullness of the air about us
Only a shocking failure to breathe
A moment without any air
Can remind us of how we need it
And what effort we must take
Only then do we relearn
And rebuild the muscles to heave
And the conversion begins again
This time with humility, grace and gratitude

The heart and the head

The heart and the head went to battle
'You'll lose' each said, 'and I'll be the one'
The head planned and mapped each move it would take
The heart sang with joy at the victory to come
The battle ensued, and how each one fought
Late into the night, the two enmeshed
The head meticulously slashed at the heart
The heart in tears pounded skull, bone and flesh
The battle blew out and darkness descended
Two parts of us all in utter defeat fell
For the head needs the heart to experience the world
The heart, the head to navigate well

Part three
It's good to talk

Me: Hello... God?

God: Hello, Jim. A new day starts.

Me: I just wanted to say thank you for this brand new day.

God: I made this day. Rejoice in that fact and be glad in the day to come.

Me: I will. I got a feeling today when I got up and looked at the sky, of the possibilities of each day.

God: I am all possibility.

Me: What has happened has happened. What is to come hasn't happened yet. But in this moment I feel alive and close to you.

God: You must have slept well! I am in all ways close to you. The moments when you allow yourself to feel that are, indeed, moments of all possibility. Use this day wisely.

Me: I will look for your path and walk close to you.

God: And I will light the way. Go...

It's good to talk.

Me: Hello...God?

God: Hello, son. I've been waiting to hear from you today.

Me: I've got some friends who are really hurting at the minute.

God: I know.

Me: They've got it really rough. One has lost a brother. Another has lost a son. Another, a job. Another has cancer. They're devastated.

God: I know.

Me: They don't know what to do.

God: I know.

Me: They're questioning whether or not you actually exist.

God: I know.

Me: Their pain is so immense.

God: I know.

Me: I don't know what to tell them. What should I say?

God: I know.

Me: What?

God: Listen to me. I.... know....

Me: Tell them you know?

God: I know. I really know. I know them. I knew them before I formed them in the womb, They are mine. I know the pain they are going through. I am with them. Whether they always know it or not, doesn't change the fact. I know. And their pain will end. I know.

Me: God knows. I'll tell them God knows.

God: I know.
It's good to talk.

Me: Hello...God?
God: Hello, Jim my son.
Me: I'm worried about someone.
God: I know. I know that person too. I know their worries. I know their anguish. I am with them in that. I know it's hard to understand- for both you and that person. But I am there.
Me: What should I do?
God: What you can. The rest? I'll take care of that.
Me: Thank you.
God: Be not afraid. For I am with you all always. Till the end of time.
It's good to talk.

Me: Hello... God?
God: Hello my son. How are you?
Me: I'm feeling old.
God: Tell me about it! No, really, tell me about it.
Me: My hair is getting whiter. My body is tired and not working like it used to. I've got friends and family who are ill and some are dead or dying.
God: Tell me. What do you see in all of that?
Me: Life is tough. There is sadness along the way. And pain.
God: Is that all? What else do you see when you look again?
Me: I see that people are kind when others are in need. I see that I hurt when others do. And want it to be better for them. I see that when others die, as well as feeling their absence, I am reminded that I am alive still and that gives me a sense of the value of my life and a better sense of perspective. I see that having a slower body means a slower life and an ability to reflect more. I see opportunity to love others in their pain. I see that. All of that. Wow!
God: So what do you see?
Me: I see that getting older means a chance for growth and wisdom, in the midst of the hardship.
God: And every day you get older, you take a step closer to me. I promise.
Me: Erm.. On that point... You know already, don't you? I mean, you know when and how I die?
God: Good night, Jim.
It's good to talk.

Me: Hello... God?

God: Hello, Jim. Good to hear from you.

Me: Yeah. Emmm. Well... I just wanted to say hello.

God: You just did that. There's something else on your mind. What is it?

Me: I.. I'm full of self doubt sometimes. I feel a bit lost.

God: Believe it or not, that's not a bad place to be.

Me: What do you mean? It feels bad.

God: I know it does. But what I mean is this. When you feel lost and you feel full of self doubt, where do you go?

Me: I usually come and talk to you.

God: And I'm always here. That's what I mean. In those times of being lost, you finally get the Way. To me.

Me: So... Do you want me to feel self doubt?

God: No! You do that all by yourself. I just want you to find me. When you search for me with all your heart, you will find me. And when you find me, you can come and rest with me and together we'll heal your self doubt.

Me: But I feel guilty sometimes only coming to you when I'm in need.

God: Don't. Guilt won't help you much.

Me: I'll try to remember to talk to you when things are going well. You know, to say thanks and all.

God: That'd be good.

Me: Because I have a lot to be thankful for. My family, my friends, my job. Lots. Come to think of it, life isn't that bad. I have connections to others. I have a purpose in my relationships with others. I play a part in your world. A small part, I know. But a part all the same. I don't do too bad, you know.

God: So about that self doubt and being lost??

Me: Thanks... Again.

It's good to talk.

Me: Hello... God?

God: Hello, Jim. How are you today?

Me: I'm OK. I've got a busy day ahead.

God: I know, remember?

Me: Oh, yeah. That's right. Omnipotent. Sorry. Anyway, I just want to take a minute to say hello in case the busyness of the day overtakes me.

God: I appreciate you doing that, Jim. You get caught up in busy days a lot, don't you?

Me: Yeah. Life can be busy. And I know that I seem to forget about our relationship quickly when I get busy.

God: I never forget about our relationship. I'm always here waiting, watching for your return.

Me: It's only when I take time to reflect on that, that I realise how amazing that is. Amazing because I'm so insignificant.

God: Not to me, you're not. Am I insignificant to you?

Me: No! But I know that I need to take more time to talk to you and I must get to know you better.

God: It's not so much that you NEED to or MUST do that. It's more that you CAN do that. You CAN know me better. You CAN come and rest in me. You CAN lay your worries and your sins down.

Me: I CAN. I can. It's more of a privileged invitation to a great feast than an obligation or burden in itself.

God: Now we're talking. Take these thoughts with you through the day. If you do, I know you will love yourself and others more; you'll tell them about the invitation (it's open to everyone by the way); and you'll realise that you CAN talk to me any time.

Me: I will. Thank you. I will walk closer to you.

God: Go. The day awaits. Talk soon.

It's good to talk.

Me: Hello... God?

God: Hello Jim. I've been listening out for you. How are you today?

Me: Don't ask...

God: I just did, son. Tell me.

Some time later...

Me: So the answer is love? To everything?

God: Yes, son. In your times of joy, I am love. You must do the same. In your times of distress, I am love. You must do the same. In times of tense relationship, I am love. You must do the same.

Me: In times of illness, God is love. In times of death, God is love. In war and peace, God is love.

God: Now you're getting it.

Me: It's hard sometimes.

God: I know. I watched my other Son, your Brother, suffer and die. I was love then too. Follow His way and keep to His path.

Me: I'll try.

God: I love a trier Keep going. I'll watch and listen out for you. Talk soon.

It's good to talk